D0055471

REGENTS RENAISSANCE DRAMA SERIES

General Editor: Cyrus Hoy
Advisory Editor: G. E. Bentley

THE CHANGELING

353796/5899559

PR
2714
C5
1966b

THOMAS MIDDLETON
and
WILLIAM ROWLEY

The Changeling

Edited by

GEORGE WALTON WILLIAMS

DISCARDED

NORMANDALE STATE JUNIOR COLLEGE
9700 FRANCE AVENUE SOUTH
BLOOMINGTON, MINNESOTA 55431

UNIVERSITY OF NEBRASKA PRESS · LINCOLN

To the Students of English 181,
Duke University, 1964–1965

Publishers on the Plains

UNP

Copyright © 1966 by the University of Nebraska Press
All Rights Reserved
Library of Congress Catalog Card Number: 65–15340

MANUFACTURED IN THE UNITED STATES OF AMERICA

Regents Renaissance Drama Series

The purpose of the Regents Renaissance Drama Series is to provide soundly edited texts, in modern spelling, of the more significant plays of the Elizabethan, Jacobean, and Caroline theater. Each text in the series is based on a fresh collation of all sixteenth- and seventeenth-century editions. The textual notes, which appear above the line at the bottom of each page, record all substantive departures from the edition used as the copy-text. Variant substantive readings among sixteenth- and seventeenth-century editions are listed there as well. In cases where two or more of the old editions present widely divergent readings, a list of substantive variants in editions through the seventeenth century is given in an appendix. Editions after 1700 are referred to in the textual notes only when an emendation originating in some one of them is received into the text. Variants of accidentals (spelling, punctuation, capitalization) are not recorded in the notes. Contracted forms of characters' names are silently expanded in speech prefixes and stage directions, and, in the case of speech prefixes, are regularized. Additions to the stage directions of the copy-text are enclosed in brackets. Stage directions such as "within" or "aside" are enclosed in parentheses when they occur in the copy-text.

Spelling has been modernized along consciously conservative lines. "Murther" has become "murder," and "burthen," "burden," but within the limits of a modernized text, and with the following exceptions, the linguistic quality of the original has been carefully preserved. The variety of contracted forms (*'em, 'am, 'm, 'um, 'hem*) used in the drama of the period for the pronoun *them* are here regularly given as *'em*, and the alternation between *a'th'* and *o'th'* (for *on* or *of the*) is regularly reproduced as *o'th'*. The copy-text distinction between preterite endings in *-d* and *-ed* is preserved except where the elision of *e* occurs in the penultimate syllable; in such cases, the final syllable is contracted. Thus, where the old editions read "threat'ned," those of the present series read "threaten'd." Where, in the old editions, a contracted preterite in *-y'd* would yield *-i'd* in modern spelling (as in "try'd," "cry'd," "deny'd"), the word is here given in its full form (e.g., "tried," "cried," "denied").

Punctuation has been brought into accord with modern practices. The effort here has been to achieve a balance between the generally light pointing of the old editions, and a system of punctuation which, without overloading the text with exclamation marks, semicolons, and dashes, will make the often loosely flowing verse (and prose) of the original syntactically intelligible to the modern reader. Dashes are regularly used only to indicate interrupted speeches, or shifts of address within a single speech.

Explanatory notes, chiefly concerned with glossing obsolete words and phrases, are printed below the textual notes at the bottom of each page. References to stage directions in the notes follow the admirable system of the Revels editions, whereby stage directions are keyed, decimally, to the line of the text before or after which they occur. Thus, a note on 0.2 has reference to the second line of the stage direction at the beginning of the scene in question. A note on 115.1 has reference to the first line of the stage direction following line 115 of the text of the relevant scene.

CYRUS HOY

University of Rochester

Contents

List of Abbreviations

Bawcutt	N. W. Bawcutt, ed. *The Changeling*. Cambridge, Mass., 1958.
corr.	corrected; i.e., the reading that results after a "stop-press" correction has been made.
Dialect Dict.	Joseph Wright. *The English Dialect Dictionary*. 6 vols. London, 1898.
Dict. of Slang	Eric Partridge. *A Dictionary of Slang*. 2 vols. London, 1961.
Dilke	Charles Wentworth Dilke, ed. *Old English Plays*. 6 vols. London, 1814–1815.
Dyce	Alexander Dyce, ed. *The Works of Thomas Middleton*. 5 vols. London, 1840.
Neilson	William Allan Neilson, ed. *Chief Elizabethan Dramatists*. Cambridge, Mass., 1911.
OED	*Oxford English Dictionary*
om.	omitted
Q	The quarto edition comprising the issues of 1653 and 1668.
S.D.	stage direction
S.P.	speech prefix
Sampson	Martin W. Sampson, ed. *Thomas Middleton*. New York, 1915.
Schelling	Felix E. Schelling and Matthew W. Black, eds. *Typical Elizabethan Plays*. New York, 1948.
Sidney	Albert Feuillerat, ed. *The Complete Works of Sir Philip Sidney*. 4 vols. Cambridge, 1912–1926.
Spencer	Hazelton Spencer. *Elizabethan Plays*. Boston, 1948.
uncorr.	uncorrected; i.e., the original reading of the type before a "stop-press" correction has been made.

Introduction

Thomas Middleton and William Rowley probably wrote *The Changeling* in the spring of 1622, for one of the literary sources of the play was entered for printing on March 11, 1622, and the play was complete on May 7, 1622, when it was licensed for performance by the company under the protection of Princess Elizabeth, Queen of Bohemia.[1] The earliest evidence for the existence of the play is this licensing:

> Licensed to be acted by the Lady Elizabeth's Servants at the Phoenix, May 7, 1622 [by Sir Henry Herbert Master of the Revels].

There is reason to believe that the play was an immediate success, as it was soon performed by the company at court.

> Upon the Sonday after, beinge the 4 of January 1623 [i.e., 1624], by the Queene of Bohemias company, *The Changelinge*, the prince only being there. Att Whitehall.

When the company disbanded during the plague of 1625, the rights to perform the play remained with Christopher Beeston, owner of the Phoenix. After the plague Queen Henrietta's Company occupied that theater and there produced the play until 1636. During the plague of that year the company reorganized and removed to the Salisbury Court Theater in Whitefriars, where it played *The Changeling* until, by command of the Lord Chamberlain, the rights to the play were denied the company and were assigned to Beeston's son William for performance by a new company then playing at the Phoenix, the King and Queen's Young Company.

The Phoenix was closed as a theater in 1642 and at some time after its closing seems to have served as a residence for a bookseller and former actor, John Rhodes. Late in 1659, when the restoration of the king was imminent, Rhodes assembled a company at the

[1] The stage history derives from G. E. Bentley, *The Jacobean and Caroline Stage* (Oxford, 1941–1956), *passim*.

Phoenix which included *The Changeling* in its repertory. This company became the Duke of York's Company; it played for a few months at the Salisbury Court Theater in Whitefriars until it transferred in June, 1661, to its new building, the Duke of York's Theater in Lincoln's Inn Fields. Samuel Pepys reports that on February 23, 1661, he went

> by water to Whitefriars to the Play-house, and there saw *The Changeling*, the first time it hath been acted these twenty years, and it takes exceedingly.

One of the reasons it "took exceedingly" was the presence in the cast of Betterton as De Flores and Sheppey as Antonio, his most famous part, one which he acted to "general satisfaction." Before Sheppey, Tim Reade had established his career as a comedian in the part of Antonio with Queen Henrietta's Company from 1637 to 1639, and William Robbins had preceded him in the part before 1636.

Other indications of the general popularity of *The Changeling* are pictorial and linguistic. The figure of a changeling appears in the frontispiece of Francis Kirkman's *The Wits* (1662) among such comic characters as Falstaff and Mrs. Quickly. The presence of this figure suggests that the mid-seventeenth century knew a farcical droll based on the comic scenes of the play. It is, furthermore, likely that the play contributed a new word to the language, for the word "tony," meaning a simpleton or fool, appears in writing in 1654 (*OED*). It remained sufficiently current to be included in Dr. Johnson's *Dictionary* (1755) and—even more remarkably—in that gentleman's polite conversation.

After many years' success on the stage, and ten years after the closing of the theaters, *The Changeling* was entered in the Stationers' Register:

> 1652 October 19: Entred [to Master Mosely] under the hands of Sr. Nath: Brent and Master Thrale warden, a comedie called The changeling, written by Rowley.[2]

Early in the next year the play was printed in quarto by Thomas Newcomb with this title page:

> The Changeling: As it was Acted (with great Applause) at the Privat house in Drury-Lane, and Salisbury Court. Written by

---

[2] *Stationers' Register* (1640–1708), I, 403; see also for the printing history W. W. Greg, *A Bibliography of the English Printed Drama to the Restoration* (London, 1939–1959), II, 828–829.

Thomas Midleton, and William Rowley. Gent'. Never printed before. London, Printed for Humphrey Moseley, and are to be sold at his shop at the sign of the Princes-Arms in St. Pauls Church-yard, 1653.

The quarto appeared also with the title page showing the variant imprint "London, Printed in the year 1653." The variant without the publisher, as Greg suggests, may have been designed for private circulation. As there are extant three copies of the quarto without the publisher's name and seven times that number with the publisher's name, it is probable that the variant without the name was the smaller and earlier state of this 1653 issue. The play was reissued in 1668, the unsold sheets being provided with a new title page canceling the one of 1653:

> The Changeling: As it was Acted (with great Applause) by the Servants of his Royal Highness the Duke of York, at the Theatre in Lincolns-Inn Fields. London, Printed for A[nne] M[oseley] and sold by Thomas Dring, at the White Lyon, over against the Inner Temple-Gate in Fleet-Street. 1668.

These two issues comprise the first edition. This edition was composed in quarto with one skeleton and (on the basis of the proportion of swash italic) from one set of cases and hence probably by one compositor. Three formes were corrected during the printing (outer B, D, G); twenty-three accidental and three substantive corrections (one of them wrongly) were made.[3] The text evidently has a high degree of substantive accuracy though there are many careless and trivial errors. It gives no specific and convincing indication of having been set from authorial foul papers or from theatrical copy (promptbook); on the basis of the survival of some linguistic preferences and of the general regularity and evenness of the quarto, one may hazard the guess that the copy was a fair scribal transcript (written in secretary hand) of the authors' foul papers, from which the promptbook would have been prepared.

No other issue or edition of the play was published in the seventeenth century. It is surprising that a play so generally well known and with so much popularity on the stage should have had so little popularity

[3] Copies of the first edition have been collated by N. W. Bawcutt, ed., *The Changeling* (Cambridge, 1958), p. xvi, and Robert C. Lawrence, "A Bibliographical Study of Middleton and Rowley's *The Changeling*," *The Library*, 5th Ser., XVI (March, 1961), 37–43.

on the shelves, but such is its history. The play was not reprinted until its inclusion in the collection of *Old English Plays* edited by C. W. Dilke in 1815; since then it has appeared in many anthologies and series.

In the quarto the play is divided into acts but not into scenes. The divisions between Acts II and III and between Acts III and IV are marked by stage business, and it is probable that on the Jacobean stage they were marked also by music. Editors have numbered the scenes. The present edition for convenience of reference follows the traditional arrangement, but it must be observed that the editorial division which occurs after III.i.10 is erroneous. There should properly be no new scene at this point; the same actors continue the same matters without interruption. Their temporary disappearance and immediate re-entry (signifying that they have changed their ground) do not constitute a scene break.

As a collaborative effort, *The Changeling* is singularly successful, the work of the two authors being so composed and organized as to leave few discrepancies or irregularities. Scholars have assigned the authorship of the several scenes on the bases of (1) textual parallels to the unaided plays of Middleton or Rowley, citing characteristic themes, images, vocabulary, and types of word-play; (2) versification, noting the proportion of feminine endings and the relative ease and flexibility of the blank verse; and (3) character types. Evidence from these criteria assigns to Rowley Acts I, III.iii, IV.iii, V.iii; and to Middleton Acts II, III.i–ii, IV.i,ii, V.i,ii.[4] The evidence from linguistic preferences has confirmed this division and has revealed a further distinction in IV.ii, giving to Rowley the opening seventeen lines of the scene, to Middleton the remaining lines.[5] This division assigns to Rowley the opening and closing scenes of the play (I.i, V.iii), the comic plot (I.ii, III.iii, IV,iii), and the lines in which Vermandero discovers the absence of two of his Gentlemen (IV.ii.1–17); and to Middleton the tragic plot (II.i,ii, III.i–ii, IV.i,ii.18–151, V.i,ii), including the lines in which Alibius reveals the location of the two Gentlemen (V.ii.49–87). The two plots and their authors are thus distinct except for the two passages where the

4 Bawcutt, pp. xxxix–xliv.
5 Cyrus Hoy, "The Shares of Fletcher and his Collaborators in the Beaumont and Fletcher Canon (V)," *Studies in Bibliography*, XIII (1960), 87–88; Oliphant had earlier conjectured the division of IV.ii but had advanced no evidence.

plots converge (each author contributes one of these passages) and the first and last scenes. In number of lines, the shares are nearly equal, though the comic plot is just half the length of the tragic plot. The influence of each author on the work of the other can be detected throughout the play.

The comic plot has presumably no specific literary source; attempts to cuckold the old husband of a young wife with or without the connivance of servants and the acquiescence of the wife are legion in their variety and legendary in their antiquity. The locating of the scenes in a private mental hospital is a device not unknown on the seventeenth-century stage, and the visits of the public, feared by the doctor, were a commonplace diversion of the period.

The tragic plot derives from two quite specific literary sources, both newly published when Middleton began to write his share of the play.[6] The main outlines of the plot are to be found in John Reynolds's *The Triumph of Gods Revenge against the Crying and Execrable Sinne of Wilful and Premeditated Murder*, entered for printing June 7, 1621, and published the same year. To this work Middleton owes the personages of Vermandero, Beatrice Joanna, Diaphanta, Alsemero, Don Alonzo and Don Tomazo Piracquo, and De Flores, and the incidents and their disposition through the murder of Piracquo (I—III.i–ii) and the marriage of Alsemero (dumbshow following Act III). The second literary source was Leonard Digges's *Gerardo the Unfortunate Spaniard*, entered for printing March 11, 1622. To this source Middleton owes the demand made by De Flores (III.iv), the events of the wedding night (V.i), and something of the spirit of De Flores. For the resolution (V.iii), Middleton and Rowley have returned for some details to Reynolds. The two sources are skilfully blended into a coherent and logical unity. The pregnancy and virginity tests (IV.i,ii) are not to be found in Mizaldus's *Secrets in Nature* (*De Arcanis Naturae*), but comparable ones appear in his *Centuriae IX. Memorabilium.*[7]

The association of the comic plot with the tragic plot may be ascribed without question to the collaborating authors, who have related the two widely disparate plots structurally, tonally, thematic-

[6] These were first pointed out by, respectively, Langbaine, *An Account of the English Dramatic Poets* (London, 1691), p. 371, and Bertram Lloyd, "A Minor Source of *The Changeling*," *Modern Language Review*, XIX (January, 1924), 101–102.

[7] Martin W. Sampson, ed. *Thomas Middleton* (New York, 1915), p. 402.

ally, and metaphorically with a subtlety and effectiveness that lets them speak as one on the unifying concept of transformation, or the condition of being a changeling.[8]

The mechanical (or narrative) link between the plots is tenuous; they are connected only by the presence of Antonio and Franciscus, Gentlemen of the household of Vermandero, in the hospital of Alibius. The plots converge structurally only three times: at IV.ii.1–17, where Vermandero discovers that the Gentlemen are missing; at V.ii.49–87, where Alibius reveals that they are found; and at V.iii.122–220, where all discoveries are finally made. They present, however, several characters in parallel, chiefly represented by the two quadrangles of Beatrice–De Flores–Piracquo–Alsemero and of Isabella–Lollio–Alibius–Antonio/Franciscus. The relationship between these parallels appears most clearly in this pattern of situations: De Flores, overhearing Beatrice and Alsemero, attempts to seduce Beatrice and so deceive her husband; Lollio, overhearing Isabella and Antonio, attempts to seduce Isabella and so deceive her husband. And in this pattern: Beatrice uses one unwanted lover (De Flores) to dispose of another (Piracquo); Isabella threatens to use one unwanted lover (Antonio) to dispose of another (Lollio).

Though the comic plot does not possess the evenness and regularity in the disposition of incidents and situations that mark the tragic plot and is therefore not a consistent commentary, there are sequences where it offers structurally its comment on the tragic plot. The confinement of Isabella by her husband (I.ii) anticipates the confinement of Beatrice by her father in the next scene and by her husband in the

---

[8] Recent criticism of *The Changeling* includes T. S. Eliot, "Thomas Middleton," *Selected Essays* (London, 1958), pp. 161–170; William Empson, *Some Versions of Pastoral* (London, 1935), pp. 48–52; M. C. Bradbrook, *Themes and Conventions of Elizabethan Tragedy* (Cambridge, 1935), pp. 213–224; Una Ellis-Fermor, *The Jacobean Drama* (London, 1958), pp. 144–149; Fredson Bowers, *Elizabethan Revenge Tragedy* (Princeton, 1940), pp. 204–206; Helen Gardner, "Milton's 'Satan' and the Theme of Damnation in Elizabethan Tragedy," *English Studies 1948* (London, 1948), pp. 55–58; Karl Holzknecht, "The Dramatic Structure of *The Changeling*," *Rennaissance Papers 1954* (Columbia, S.C., 1955), pp. 77–87; Samuel Schoenbaum, *Middleton's Tragedies* (New York, 1955), pp. 132–149; Richard Hindry Barker, *Thomas Middleton* (New York, 1958), pp. 121–131; N. W. Bawcutt, ed., *The Changeling*, pp. xlv–lxviii; Christopher Ricks, "The Moral and Poetic Structure of *The Changeling*," *Essays in Criticism*, X (July, 1960), 290–306; Edward Engelberg, "Tragic Blindness in *The Changeling* and *Women Beware Women*," *Modern Language Quarterly*, XXIII (March, 1962), 20–28.

fifth act. The seduction offer made by Lollio (III.iii) anticipates the seduction offer made by De Flores in the next scene. The revelation of Vermandero's suspects for murder is juxtaposed with that of Alsemero's proofs. These anticipations, repetitions, and juxtapositions of identical or parallel characters and situations unify the two plots structurally. The comic plot by means of the transformations of its changelings reflects in another mode the perplexities of the tragic plot created by the transformations of its changelings. By providing differing points of view for similar or comparable situations, the comic and tragic plots collaborate to enrich the play thematically.

A specific function of the comic plot is the evocation of a tone of sexuality and lasciviousness. The sexual meanings of the violent episode of the glove in the tragic plot (I.i.221–233), for example, will hardly be missed, but the comic plot drives them home by repeating the same verb in a similar context (I.ii.26–31). The comic plot continually invites the audience to be sensitive to *double-entendre* and innuendo. Double meanings are intimated more appropriately and with greater decorum in the comic than in the tragic plot, but it is in the latter that they have impressive force.

The thematic interrelation of the two plots is evident in the ramifications of meaning afforded by the title of the play. The denotation of the word "changeling" familiar to a modern audience is "an infant exchanged by fairies for another infant"; it is the only meaning not relevant to the play. A changeling for this play is a waverer or a fickle person, a person surreptitiously put in exchange for another, or an idiot (*OED*). All of these meanings are relevant to one or more of the characters of the play, and all involve the concept of transformation.

In the tragic plot, Alsemero and Beatrice are the central waverers. The first action of the play is Alsemero's change of plans. Though he thinks of himself as constant (I.i.35), he changes his mind twice in the first two hundred lines of the play (ll. 51–53; 194–195). The wind vane is a fit symbol for his irresolution. The opening sequence, indeed, presents the quality of changeableness as the major theme of the play and provides an excellent background and preparation for the fickleness of the most notable changeling, Beatrice. It is her changes that impel the tragedy. Her first change is from loving Piracquo to loving Alsemero. Her second change is from loving Alsemero to loving De Flores, and her third change is from loathing De Flores to loving him. These last two changes are the crux of the tragedy; they have two particular aspects: the loss of Alsemero and the gain of De Flores. It is clear that Beatrice wishes to marry Alsemero and be his wife right up to the end of the play, but it is not clear that she loves him for so long. Her conversation turns from love to possession, and her first action after her marriage is one not of love but of mistrust, fear, and deceit. Her reference to love in the final scene is not of her love to Alsemero but of his to her (V.iii.65–66)—the tone is almost one of blame—and she is concerned to "assure" Alsemero to her (l. 72). At the same time, the gain of De Flores is described in terms of love: "I'm forc'd to love thee now," "who would not love him?" "Here's a man worth loving" (V.i.47, 71, 76). Beatrice has, it would seem, an innate affinity to De Flores; the violence of her antipathy in the opening scenes (the episode of the glove is not found in the sources) suggests that the strength of her feeling is more to be noted than its direction. De Flores's foul visage springs instantly to her mind when she contemplates murder and never leaves. "There's scarce a thing but is both lov'd and loath'd," says Alsemero (I.i.121), and the dramatist suggests in the paradox Conrad's "fascination of the abomination." Beatrice is the chief changeling of the play; her changeableness, excited by her lust, brings on her tragedy which, as T. S. Eliot has observed, lies not in the fact that she has lost Alsemero but in that she has gained De Flores.

The two arresting scenes of the play are II.ii, in which the changeling Beatrice engages the services of the constant De Flores for murder, and III.iv, in which De Flores returns for payment. In them it is possible to trace the workings of Beatrice's mind. It is a mind that holds only one idea at a time; it never proceeds to consequences. It is not aware of subtleties; Beatrice never apprehends in either scene that words have two meanings, that *service, deed,* and *blood* mean one thing to her and something else to De Flores. Beatrice describes another trait of her mind, forgetfulness:

> Oh, I was
> Lost in this small disturbance and forgot
> Affliction's fiercer torrent that now comes
> To bear down all my comforts. (II.i.93–96)

She is oblivious to external matters; she becomes lost in the thought of murder and forgets the attention due to the reimbursement for it. She allows De Flores in II.ii to postpone the specification of the payment until after the event; it is a tragic mistake. De Flores, the permanence of whose ugliness (II.ii.76–77) symbolizes that he is no changeling but a man fixed in his purposes, takes advantage of it. In III.iv, Beatrice cannot understand his demand and charges him with forgetfulness, but he knows her better than she knows herself:

> Take you heed first [of forgetfulness];
> Faith, y'are grown much forgetful. . . .
> (III.iv.96–97)

She yields to him with grief that she has lost her honor and that her "art" and clever planning have miscarried. Her yielding is the price she pays for understanding her dilemma: "Murder, I see, is followed by more sins" (III.iv.164).

Murder is followed by more sins: fornication, spying, trespassing, lying, duplicity, bribery, procuring, conspiracy, and adultery. Beatrice has become accustomed to crime. The fullness of her criminal nature and her continuing readiness to sin appear in her premeditation of the murder of Diaphanta, which thus indicates the degradation she has suffered without being fully aware of it. It further symbolizes the completeness of her union with De Flores, for both guilty partners independently reach the conclusion that Diaphanta must die. Totally submissive to his will, Beatrice accedes to De Flores's plan with no protest.

After the fire and the murder of Diaphanta, Beatrice has a few moments of success; her schemes and De Flores's actions have brought her her desires. How the triangle is to be maintained for the future does not disturb her in the least. She becomes overconfident and careless; next day she is indiscreet in her choice of a trysting place with De Flores; Alsemero observes her adulterous affection, and the catastrophe is upon her. Her last long speech testifies to the final tragic awareness which has come to her:

> Oh, come not near me, sir; I shall defile you.
> I am that of your blood was taken from you
> For your better health; look no more upon't
> But cast it to the ground regardlessly. . . .
> Beneath the stars, upon yon meteor
> Ever hung my fate 'mongst things corruptible;
> I ne'er could pluck it from him. My loathing
> Was prophet to the rest but ne'er believ'd;
> Mine honor fell with him and now my life.
> (V.iii.150–159)

Beatrice's character, the most fully and finely drawn in the drama, is supported by the character of Diaphanta, whose career is parallel to that of her mistress. Diaphanta is approached by Jasperino, who pretends "honest love, and she deserves it" (IV.ii.91). It is obvious from the first sparring that the emphasis in their association is to be physical, and Diaphanta's countenancing Jasperino's obscene banter proves that she is a lustful person. Though she is being courted in honest love, she sells herself to supply the place of her mistress. So sweet was the bargain, so gratifying to her lust, that she forgot herself—and her mistress. Diaphanta's attitude to her experiences of the wedding night the dramatist has anticipated: "But one swig more" (IV.i.115). The indulgence of the flesh cost this substitute changeling her life. The drama of Diaphanta is thus a comment on the tragedy of Beatrice, and the parallels suggest that the quality of the love the women have for their men is similar. The dramatists imply the nature of Beatrice's love by depicting that of Diaphanta.

Through the comic plot dance other changelings. Antonio, the character from whom the title of the play ostensibly derives, is labeled in the Dramatis Personae as "The Changeling," but Franciscus is as much of a changeling—an idiot—as Antonio. Alibius is seen at the conclusion of the play as one who must change to a better life, and even Isabella changes outwardly into the dress of a madwoman. But Isabella is not a changeling; in her constancy she acts as the necessary foil to Beatrice. Where Beatrice is changeable, Isabella is fixed; where Beatrice is naïve, Isabella is shrewd; where Beatrice fails, Isabella succeeds.

The heroines of the two plots embody aspects of another theme of consequence in the play, appearance and reality. Isabella is confronted with two lovers who don the clothing of fool and madman in order to accomplish their purposes; her sanity penetrates their disguises and exposes their reality. Their exposure yields them a comic wisdom; they both recognize the errors in their pretense. Such a recognition admits that the disguises have not been pretense but fact: in putting on fool's costume and becoming a changeling, Antonio has not covered his sanity but revealed his folly: "I was chang'd too from a little ass as I was to a great fool as I am" (V.iii.205–206). Franciscus acknowledges that he is as guilty (ll. 208–209). In the contrasting situation, when Isabella dons the habit of a frantic, her appearance of madness covers the reality of her saneness. She is a "feigner" come to abuse Antonio.

These deceiving costumes in the comic plot reproduce more serious elements in the tragic plot: the ugliness of De Flores and the beauty of Beatrice.

The Elizabethans believed in a psychology which held that an ugly, deformed, or misshapen body betokened an ugly soul: the crooked body of Richard III was an obvious sign of his crooked soul. The figure of De Flores is surely in the same tradition. The ugliness of De Flores's face—mentioned frequently in the play—is certain testimony of the ugliness of his soul; honest, honest De Flores, like Iago, manages to conceal that inner ugliness by calculated affability, capability, and helpfulness, but the ugliness remains. There should be no surprise that he is a murderer and ravisher; like the fool's costume, his appearance reveals his reality.

Beatrice's beauty, one would expect, would then represent a beautiful soul; it does not. Like Isabella's disguise, it is a feigning; it conceals her real nature, one that is close to the ugliness of De Flores. The identity of their natures insures that Beatrice will act as like De Flores in lust as she has thought like him in planning to murder Diaphanta. The disguise of Isabella is a harmless one, put on to set all right; the disguise of Beatrice is hypocrisy, and from it nothing can come but harm. The hypocrisy of Beatrice is another of the themes of the play, most fully stated in the fifth act where the mask of modesty is removed from the ugliness of her cunning. Beatrice puts the matter into words herself, failing to understand the hypocritical implication of her speech, when she says of De Flores: "Why, put case I loath'd him . . . / Must I needs show it? Cannot I keep that secret . . . ?" (II.ii.66–68). The deceiving of De Flores here prepares for the deceiving of Alsemero later: "I'm put now to my cunning; th' effects I know, / If I can now but feign 'em handsomely" (IV.ii.138–139). Neither deception succeeds: for the failure of the first Beatrice pays with her honor; for the failure of the second, with her life.

Partly because hypocrisy is the evil that walks invisible, the play is rich in metaphors of sight and references to the eyes. The first line directs attention to Alsemero's sight of Beatrice, and Beatrice's first long speech is a commentary on sight in its relation to judgment:

> Our eyes are sentinels unto our judgments
> And should give certain judgment what they see,
> But they are rash sometimes and tell us wonders
> Of common things, which when our judgments find,
> They can then check the eyes and call them blind.
>
> (I.i.69–73)

The facility of this speech and its triteness, with Beatrice's glib assurance in giving the conventional amatory check to Alsemero's impetuosity, reveal her need for the wisdom of an observation she hardly understands even though she speaks it. The first mistake that Beatrice detects in her eyes is their judgment of Piracquo: "Sure, mine eyes were mistaken," (l. 81) she decides after they have glimpsed Alsemero. Almost immediately following this speech, "Enter De Flores" speaking of the instruction the eye can give: "Your eye shall instantly instruct you" (l. 90). The arrival of De Flores at this precise moment is an ironic dramatic comment on Beatrice's discovery of the first error of her eyes. To Beatrice's eyes, De Flores is poison as deadly as the basilisk (ll. 108, 111), and Tomazo seconds her in this judgment (V.ii.18). Poison, however, can serve as a medicative. Beatrice discovers that poison can cure through the prescription of her "art" (II.ii.46–47), and she sees De Flores as one poison which will expel another, Piracquo. Her eye does not instruct her that, though used as a curative, poison is still poison and while curing one ill demands a cure for itself. This elementary truth the comic plot twice presents in Franciscus's speech to his doctor, Lollio. The jibberish of the spider and the whip yields relevant comment. Franciscus warns that "there's a spider in the cup; no, 'tis but a grapestone; swallow it, fear nothing" (III.iii.40–41). The object in the cup is reassuringly not a poisonous spider, merely a grapestone, but this particular grapestone was as lethal as poison. Not many lines later, Franciscus addresses Lollio: "Aesculapius, hide the poison" (l. 61). The whip is hidden from sight, but it is always present and it reappears to punish once more (ll. 85–86).

Beatrice's eyes judge wrongly about De Flores again:

> His face loathes one,
> But look upon his care, who would not love him?
> (V.i.70–71)

Beatrice, having seen with intellectual eyesight (II.i.19) the beauty of Alsemero, here attempts to see the inner beauty of De Flores and to love him for his care. She is mistaken again; De Flores has no inner beauty. (Poison is still poison.) De Flores's "care" is selfish, his pleasure and continuance. The pity of it in this pitiless play is that, by Act V, De Flores's inner ugliness (which is his care for himself) has come to be for Beatrice an adequate beauty. That inadequate vision includes Beatrice's seeing that murder is followed by more sins: evil proliferates unpredictably. No amount of poison, no number of poisons, will cure permanently; clear vision requires the denial of sight to Vermandero:

> I am that of your blood was taken from you
> For your better health; look no more upon't . . . .

As the pattern of sight imagery involves images of poison closely related to it, so the dramatists similarly interweave other patterns. The image of health and blood-letting in Beatrice's last long speech concludes another significant pattern. Beatrice has seen her deformity in these lines, recognizing the ailment that Jasperino had already diagnosed as an "ulcer . . . / Full of corruption" (V.iii.8–9). She admits that she has contaminated her father, but both Alsemero and De Flores have already testified to the fact that she has infected them. Alsemero describes his love for Beatrice as "some hidden malady / Within me that I understand not" (I.i.24–25), and De Flores complains of "lovers' plagues" (III.iv.151) and a "mad qualm" (II.i.79). Beatrice terms her loathing for De Flores her infirmity; such it proves to be—"prophet to the rest." The imagery of sickness emanating from Beatrice—another basilisk (IV.ii.107)—correlates with the presence of many "physicians" in the play. Alsemero is an amateur physician; Alibius is a professional. Beatrice and Isabella stand once again in structural opposition in the two plots. Beatrice vainly fancies herself a doctor: she would cure De Flores's ugliness (the appearance that cannot be cured or changed), she would cure Alsemero's sickness by lies and hypocrisy (V.iii.15–18). Reality and truth frustrate both cures, but Isabella "can cure fools and madmen" (IV.iii.31–32).

In an interchange at the beginning of the play (I.i.133–147), Jasperino professes himself a physician and prescribes for his madness the cure of love. Diaphanta directs him to Alibius, the only genuine doctor in the play. This interchange serves many functions. It delineates the character of Diaphanta as unashamedly lustful and thus prepares for the misadventures of V.i. It serves as a coarse foil to the polite love-making of Alsemero and Beatrice and thus associates the immodesty of Diaphanta with the "modesty" of Beatrice. It unites the metaphor of sickness to the concept of madness and suggests that the madness of lovers is not far from the madness of madmen. It advances two herbs as medicatives, the poppy and the cuckoo. Both of them have erotic connotations, but the cuckoo is as well a remedy for diseases of the brain.

The cuckoo returns in its familiar reference to cuckoldry in the comic plot. When Lollio overhears Antonio making his proposition to Isabella, he mutters from his hiding place, "Cuckoo, cuckoo" (III.iii.187). The instantaneous dramatic response is the entrance of the madmen as birds and beasts. The juxtaposition of Antonio's proposition, Lollio's comment, and the entry of the madmen (this is their first appearance) is the powerful and spectacular device the dramatists use to say forcefully that sexual irregularities are madness and to represent through the symbol of the insane the bestiality of the sane. The entrance recalls Isabella to her senses—"Of fear enough to part us" (l. 188)—and thereafter her marriage bond is secure. Dr. Alibius can cure the madness of the brain, but only Isabella in her realistic sanity can cure the madness of the loins. She administers her cure to the fool (IV.iii.100–133) and brings him to an awareness of his folly. Isabella's success springs from her ability to control her own affections; it is quite beyond the capabilities of the changeable Beatrice. If Piracquo's acquiescence is "love's tame madness" (II.i.153), then it is love's fierce madness that Beatrice must suffer.

An interchange in the comic plot (III.iii.63–84) clinches the bond between love and madness. The passage begins with a reference to Tiresias (an archetypal changeling) whom Juno struck blind. It thus associates blindness with changeableness and provides a comment on Beatrice's early opinion of her own clear-sighted judgment: "A woman," says Lollio, "has an eye more than a man"; this may be true of Isabella in the comic plot, but it is not applicable to Beatrice. The passage concludes with a reference to Luna who has made Franciscus mad and brought him in love. Hence, it is impossible to distinguish between lover and madman in Franciscus's letter; as Lollio sees, the lover is mad still.

Is it indeed the "opacous . . . moon/ That last chang'd on us" (V.iii.197–198) that is to be blamed for the love and madness that have changed the changelings of the play? The blame cannot be so easily shifted. The moon is merely one of the omens that invest the play, and they are "but imaginary" (I.i.3), as Alsemero knows. The moon is changeable, like Beatrice; like Beatrice, the moon in this play is not chaste but lustful—the mistress of Endymion and "big-bellied." The moon does not control the flood and ebb of this tragedy; that office is reserved for her lustful counterpart on earth.

Another metaphor found in both plots describes the madness of the play in different terms—in terms of confinement. Beatrice pictures her perplexity at the condition to which her changes have brought her by saying: "I'm in a labyrinth" (III.iv.72). The image of the Minoan maze aptly describes the predicament of Beatrice who, like Daedalus, has contrived a prison in which she is herself imprisoned. The choice of the image is ironic, for Beatrice is as yet unaware that she has fashioned her own ruin; to this wisdom she comes only in the last act. Then it is too late to extricate herself from the maze that confines her. The comic plot offers its comment on this speech by having Isabella repeat the metaphor in her feigned madness:

> And let us tread the lower labyrinth;
> I'll bring thee to the clue.
> (IV.iii.105–106)

The difference between the heroines stands out clearly: Beatrice, thinking herself clearheaded, a woman of "art" (II.ii.46), has produced the madness from which she cannot escape. Isabella, feigning madness, produces a maze to which (like Ariadne) she knows the secrets. The labyrinth thus represents order and disorder. A maze is a highly artificial and ordered contrivance to those who are sane; to those who are mad it is baffling in the extreme. In this duality it suggests the locations of the two plots, their tones and contexts. The visible dramatic symbols of the duality are the marriage and the masque. Beatrice's world is one of sanity; she inhabits a sophisticated and organized society of which the fitting representation is the marriage. The marriage is an expression of happiness and harmony— or rather it ought to be, but based impossibly on murder it denies harmony. As a consequence, it cannot be consummated: it is no marriage. Beatrice's madness destroys her world of sanity. Isabella's world is one of madness; she is surrounded by a cacophonous and disordered society the fitting representation of which is the masque (IV.iii.208.1–2). The masque, more accurately an anti-masque of madmen and fools, expresses confusion and disharmony. Isabella joins this confusion by dressing in the habit of a frantic, but her sanity overcomes her world of madness.

The tragic plot advanced the metaphor of the labyrinth to describe the world of madness, and the comic plot responded by offering the escape from that madness. Another image of confinement is advanced by the comic plot in the game of barley-break; the tragic plot responds to it by demonstrating that there is no escape. After Antonio has confessed his love to Isabella, Lollio offers to take him away. Isabella, pleased by his protestation of affection, answers, "By no means; let him stay a little" (III.iii.161). Unwittingly, the madmen scream their comment on her acquiescence: "Catch the last couple in hell." The merest intimation of adultery provokes the intrusion of this symbolic game. The madmen themselves appear in a few lines, and Isabella rejects Antonio finally. When it is mentioned in the tragic plot, the game brings with it the horror and madness of the comic bedlam. It occurs as De Flores confesses the adultery:

> I coupled with your mate
> At barley-break; now we are left in hell.
> (V.iii.163–164)

Murder is followed by more sins, of which the chief is adultery, the pilot which will guide the lovers to the bottomless pit. For Beatrice and De Flores there is no escape from madness; they are left in hell.

GEORGE WALTON WILLIAMS

Duke University

THE CHANGELING

Dramatis Personae

VERMANDERO, *father to Beatrice*
TOMAZO DE PIRACQUO, *a noble lord*
ALONZO DE PIRACQUO, *his brother, suitor to Beatrice*
ALSEMERO, *a nobleman, afterwards married to Beatrice*
JASPERINO, *his friend*
ALIBIUS, *a jealous doctor*
LOLLIO, *his man*
PEDRO, *friend to Antonio*
ANTONIO, *the changeling* [*the counterfeit fool*]
FRANCISCUS, *the counterfeit madman*
DE FLORES, *servant to Vermandero*
MADMEN [AND FOOLS]
SERVANTS

BEATRICE [JOANNA], *daughter to Vermandero*
DIAPHANTA, *her waiting-woman*
ISABELLA, *wife to Alibius*

The Scene: *Alicant*

-2-

The Changeling

[I.i]   *Enter* Alsemero.

ALSEMERO.

 'Twas in the temple where I first beheld her,
 And now again the same; what omen yet
 Follows of that? None but imaginary.
 Why should my hopes or fate be timorous?
 The place is holy, so is my intent;   5
 I love her beauties to the holy purpose
 And that, methinks, admits comparison
 With man's first creation, the place blest,
 And is his right home back, if he achieve it.
 The church hath first begun our interview   10
 And that's the place must join us into one;
 So there's beginning and perfection too.

                    Enter Jasperino.

JASPERINO.

 Oh, sir, are you here? Come, the wind's fair with you;
 Y'are like to have a swift and pleasant passage.

ALSEMERO.

 Sure y'are deceived, friend; 'tis contrary   15
 In my best judgment.

JASPERINO.   What, for Malta?

 If you could buy a gale amongst the witches,

Changeling] For comments on the significance of the title, see the Introduction, p. xv.

 6. *holy purpose*] marriage.

 8. *the place*] Paradise.

 12. *beginning and perfection*] The circle has traditionally been regarded as the symbol of perfection and permanence.

 17. *buy a gale*] a reference to the superstition that witches controlled the winds; see Webster and Rowley, *A Cure for a Cuckold*, IV.ii.97, and *Macbeth*, I.iii.11.

They could not serve you such a lucky pennyworth
As comes o' God's name.

ALSEMERO.   Even now I observ'd
The temple's vane to turn full in my face;   20
I know 'tis against me.

JASPERINO.   Against you?
Then you know not where you are.

ALSEMERO.   Not well indeed.

JASPERINO.
Are you not well, sir?

ALSEMERO.   Yes, Jasperino,
Unless there be some hidden malady
Within me that I understand not.

JASPERINO.   And that   25
I begin to doubt, sir; I never knew
Your inclinations to travels at a pause
With any cause to hinder it, till now.
Ashore you were wont to call your servants up
And help to trap your horses for the speed;   30
At sea I have seen you weigh the anchor with 'em,
Hoist sails for fear to lose the foremost breath,
Be in continual prayers for fair winds;
And have you chang'd your orisons?

ALSEMERO.   No, friend,
I keep the same church, same devotion.   35

JASPERINO.
Lover I'm sure y'are none, the stoic
Was found in you long ago; your mother
Nor best friends who have set snares of beauty
(Ay, and choice ones too) could never trap you that way.
What might be the cause?

ALSEMERO.   Lord, how violent   40
Thou art. I was but meditating of
Somewhat I heard within the temple.

---

19. *o' God's name*] as the gift of God.
20. *temple's vane*] the wind-vane atop the temple; though it circumscribes
a circle, it is the symbol of change and impermanence.
26. *doubt*] fear.
30. *trap*] dress with trappings.
30. *for the speed*] to hasten matters.

JASPERINO.
  Is this violence? 'Tis but idleness
  Compar'd with your haste yesterday.
ALSEMERO.
  I'm all this while a-going, man.   45

                    Enter Servants.

JASPERINO.
  Backwards, I think, sir. Look, your servants.
FIRST SERVANT.
  The seamen call; shall we board your trunks?
ALSEMERO.
  No, not today.
JASPERINO.   'Tis the critical day
  It seems, and the sign in Aquarius.
SECOND SERVANT.
  We must not to sea today; this smoke will bring forth fire.   50
ALSEMERO.
  Keep all on shore. I do not know the end,
  Which needs I must do, of an affair in hand
  Ere I can go to sea.
FIRST SERVANT.
  Well, your pleasure.
SECOND SERVANT.
  Let him e'en take his leisure too, we are safer on land.   55
                                          Exeunt Servants.

      Enter Beatrice Joanna, Diaphanta, *and Servants.*

JASPERINO [*aside*].
  How now! The laws of the Medes are chang'd sure. Salute a
  woman? He kisses too; wonderful! Where learnt he this?
  And does it perfectly too; in my conscience he ne'er rehears'd

55.2. Beatrice . . . *Servants.*]   *Dilke*;
Beatrice, Diaphanta, and Servants,
Joannna. Q.

---

  49. *Aquarius*] the water-carrier in the zodiac; hence, a favorable time
for a sea voyage.
  50. *smoke . . . fire*] i.e., the delay is more significant than it seems; cf.
"where there's smoke, there's fire."
  56. *laws of the Medes*] unchangeable laws; Daniel 6:8.
  58. *in my conscience*] truly.

it before. Nay, go on, this will be stranger and better news at
Valencia than if he had ransom'd half Greece from the Turk.   60
BEATRICE.
You are a scholar, sir.
ALSEMERO.   A weak one, lady.
BEATRICE.
Which of the sciences is this love you speak of?
ALSEMERO.
From your tongue I take it to be music.
BEATRICE.
You are skilful in't, can sing at first sight.
ALSEMERO.
And I have show'd you all my skill at once.   65
I want more words to express me further
And must be forc'd to repetition:
I love you dearly.
BEATRICE.   Be better advis'd, sir.
Our eyes are sentinels unto our judgments
And should give certain judgment what they see,   70
But they are rash sometimes and tell us wonders
Of common things, which when our judgments find,
They can then check the eyes and call them blind.
ALSEMERO.
But I am further, lady; yesterday
Was mine eyes' employment, and hither now   75
They brought my judgment where are both agreed.
Both houses then consenting, 'tis agreed;
Only there wants the confirmation
By the hand royal; that's your part, lady.
BEATRICE.
Oh, there's one above me, sir. —[*Aside.*]   For five days past 80

---

60. *ransom'd . . . Turk*] Greece was at this time under the dominion of
Turkey.

64. *sing . . . sight*] sight-read music.

77–79. *Both . . . lady*] The metaphor is legislative; both houses of
parliament (the senses and the intellect) have approved the bill; it now
needs only the queen's signature to make it law.

80. *one*] her father or, perhaps, God.

80. *five days*] Presumably, Beatrice was engaged to Alonzo only five days
ago.

To be recall'd! Sure, mine eyes were mistaken;
This was the man was meant me. That he should come
So near his time, and miss it!
JASPERINO [*aside*].
We might have come by the carriers from Valencia, I see,
and sav'd all our sea-provision; we are at farthest sure. Me-   85
thinks I should do something too; I meant to be a venturer
in this voyage. Yonder's another vessel, I'll board her; if
she be lawful prize, down goes her topsail.

Enter De Flores.

DE FLORES.
     Lady, your father—
BEATRICE.   Is in health, I hope.
DE FLORES.
     Your eye shall instantly instruct you, lady;   90
     He's coming hitherward.
BEATRICE.   What needed then
     Your duteous preface? I had rather
     He had come unexpected; you must stall
     A good presence with unnecessary blabbing,
     And how welcome for your part you are,   95
     I'm sure you know.
DE FLORES [*aside*].   Will't never mend, this scorn,
     One side nor other? Must I be enjoin'd
     To follow still whilst she flies from me? Well,
     Fates do your worst, I'll please myself with sight
     Of her at all opportunities   100
     If but to spite her anger. I know she had

96. Will't] *Dilke*; Wilt *Q*.

---

82. *the man . . . me*] In Reynolds's account, Beatrice steadily resisted the
attentions of Alonzo; in the play, she had been in love with him.
     84. *carriers*] land transport.
     85. *at farthest*] at the farthest point from our plan.
     87. *board her*] come alongside and put my forces aboard her.
     88. *lawful prize*] i.e., a vessel which no regulations prohibit him from
capturing.
     88. *down . . . topsail*] i.e., the sign of a ship's surrender.
     93. *stall*] forestall.
     97. *One . . . other*] One way or another.

Rather see me dead than living, and yet
She knows no cause for't but a peevish will.

ALSEMERO.

You seem'd displeas'd, lady, on the sudden.

BEATRICE.

Your pardon, sir, 'tis my infirmity;   105
Nor can I other reason render you
Than his or hers, of some particular thing
They must abandon as a deadly poison,
Which to a thousand other tastes were wholesome.
Such to mine eyes is that same fellow there,   110
The same that report speaks of the basilisk.

ALSEMERO.

This is a frequent frailty in our nature.
There's scarce a man amongst a thousand found
But hath his imperfection: one distastes
The scent of roses, which to infinites   115
Most pleasing is and odoriferous;
One oil, the enemy of poison;
Another wine, the cheerer of the heart
And lively refresher of the countenance.
Indeed this fault, if so it be, is general;   120
There's scarce a thing but is both lov'd and loath'd.
Myself, I must confess, have the same frailty.

BEATRICE.

And what may be your poison, sir? I am bold with you.

ALSEMERO.

What might be your desire perhaps, a cherry.

BEATRICE.

I am no enemy to any creature   125
My memory has but yon gentleman.

ALSEMERO.

He does ill to tempt your sight, if he knew it.

107. of] *Dilke*; or *Q*.   124. What] *Dilke*; And what *Q*.
113. found] *Dilke*; sound *Q*. *See*
Appendix A.

---

107. *of*] concerning.
111. *basilisk*] an imaginary beast whose look could kill.
117. *oil*] a medicinal unction.

BEATRICE.

    He cannot be ignorant of that, sir;
    I have not spar'd to tell him so, and I want
    To help myself, since he's a gentleman   130
    In good respect with my father and follows him.

ALSEMERO.

    He's out of his place then now.   [*They talk apart.*]

JASPERINO.

    I am a mad wag, wench.

DIAPHANTA.

    So methinks; but for your comfort I can tell you we have a
    doctor in the city that undertakes the cure of such.   135

JASPERINO.

    Tush, I know what physic is best for the state of mine own
    body.

DIAPHANTA.

    'Tis scarce a well-govern'd state, I believe.

JASPERINO.

    I could show thee such a thing with an ingredient that we
    two would compound together, and if it did not tame the 140
    maddest blood i'th' town for two hours after, I'll ne'er
    profess physic again.

DIAPHANTA.

    A little poppy, sir, were good to cause you sleep.

JASPERINO.

    Poppy! I'll give thee a pop i'th' lips for that first and begin
    there. [*Kisses her.*] Poppy is one simple indeed and cuckoo 145
    (what you call't) another. I'll discover no more now; another
    time I'll show thee all.

        Enter Vermandero *and Servants.*

147.1.] *after* father, sir. (*l.* 148)
in Q.

---

    129. *want*] lack the means.
    134–135. *a doctor*] Alibius.
    136. *physic*] medicine.
    143. *poppy*] an opiate.
    145. *simple*] medicinal herb.
    145. *cuckoo*] Of the many different cuckoo flowers, two are probably
intended: (1) the cuckoo pintle-root (*arum maculatum*), described by Rowley
as "those long upright things that grow a yard above the ground" (*All's*

BEATRICE.
    My father, sir.
VERMANDERO.   Oh, Joanna, I came to meet thee.
    Your devotion's ended?
BEATRICE.   For this time, sir. —
    [*Aside.*] I shall change my saint, I fear me; I find   150
    A giddy turning in me. —Sir, this while
    I am beholding to this gentleman
    Who left his own way to keep me company,
    And in discourse I find him much desirous
    To see your castle. He hath deserv'd it, sir,   155
    If ye please to grant it.
VERMANDERO.   With all my heart, sir.
    Yet there's an article between; I must know
    Your country. We use not to give survey
    Of our chief strengths to strangers; our citadels
    Are plac'd conspicuous to outward view   160
    On promonts' tops, but within are secrets.
ALSEMERO.
    A Valencian, sir.
VERMANDERO.   A Valencian?
    That's native, sir; of what name, I beseech you?
ALSEMERO.
    Alsemero, sir.
VERMANDERO.   Alsemero? Not the son
    Of John de Alsemero?
ALSEMERO.   The same, sir.   165
VERMANDERO.
    My best love bids you welcome.
BEATRICE [*aside*].   He was wont
    To call me so, and then he speaks a most
    Unfeigned truth.
VERMANDERO.   Oh, sir, I knew your father.
    We two were in acquaintance long ago

Lost by Lust, III.iii.107); (2) the ladies' smocks (*cardamine pratensis*), traditionally used as a cure for madness.
    150. *saint*] the saint she prays to (but cf. its special significance at V.iii.52).
    158. *use*] are accustomed.
    161. *promonts'*] promontories'.
    167. *To call me so*] To call me "my best love."

Before our chins were worth iulan down   170
And so continued till the stamp of time
Had coin'd us into silver. Well, he's gone;
A good soldier went with him.

ALSEMERO.

You went together in that, sir.

VERMANDERO.

No, by Saint Jacques, I came behind him;   175
Yet I have done somewhat too. An unhappy day
Swallowed him at last at Gibraltar
In fight with those rebellious Hollanders,
Was it not so?

ALSEMERO.   Whose death I had reveng'd
Or followed him in fate, had not the late league   180
Prevented me.

VERMANDERO.   Ay, ay, 'twas time to breathe.
Oh, Joanna, I should ha' told thee news,
I saw Piracquo lately.

BEATRICE [aside].   That's ill news.

VERMANDERO.

He's hot preparing for this day of triumph;
Thou must be a bride within this sevennight.   185

ALSEMERO [aside].

Ha!

BEATRICE.

Nay, good sir, be not so violent; with speed
I cannot render satisfaction

---

170. *iulan down*] youthful fuzz; "iulan" (trisyllabic) is an adjective coined
from the name of Iulus Ascanius, the young son of Aeneas. Bawcutt points
out that Servius' commentary on the *Aeneid* derives the name from Greek
ίουλος, "the first growth of the beard."

174. *went together*] were his equal.

175. *Saint Jacques*] the patron saint of Spain, Santiago.

176–181. *An unhappy . . . breathe*] The senior Alsemero was drowned in
the battle of Gibraltar, April 25, 1607, where the Dutch (then under the
dominion of Spain) defeated a Spanish fleet. The Spanish, hard-pressed
and suffering defeats in the Indies as well, were content ("time to breathe")
to conclude a treaty on April 9, 1609 ("the late league"), which provided
for a twelve years' truce with Holland. This reference serves to date the
time of the play closely.

185. *sevennight*] week.

Unto the dear companion of my soul,
Virginity, whom I thus long have liv'd with,   190
And part with it so rude and suddenly.
Can such friends divide never to meet again
Without a solemn farewell?

VERMANDERO.   Tush, tush, there's a toy.

ALSEMERO [aside].
I must now part and never meet again
With any joy on earth. —Sir, your pardon,   195
My affairs call on me.

VERMANDERO.   How, sir? By no means;
Not chang'd so soon, I hope? You must see my castle
And her best entertainment ere we part;
I shall think myself unkindly us'd else.
Come, come, let's on; I had good hope your stay   200
Had been a while with us in Alicant;
I might have bid you to my daughter's wedding.

ALSEMERO [aside].
He means to feast me and poisons me beforehand.—
I should be dearly glad to be there, sir,
Did my occasions suit as I could wish.   205

BEATRICE.
I shall be sorry if you be not there
When it is done, sir, but not so suddenly.

VERMANDERO.
I tell you, sir, the gentleman's complete,
A courtier and a gallant, enrich'd
With many fair and noble ornaments;   210
I would not change him for a son-in-law
For any he in Spain, the proudest he,
And we have great ones, that you know.

ALSEMERO.   He's much
Bound to you, sir.

VERMANDERO.   He shall be bound to me
As fast as this tie can hold him; I'll want   215
My will else.

---

193. *toy*] trifle.
208. *complete*] i.e., "perfect."

BEATRICE [aside].   I shall want mine if you do it.
VERMANDERO.
   But come, by the way I'll tell you more of him.
ALSEMERO [aside].
   How shall I dare to venture in his castle
   When he discharges murderers at the gate?
   But I must on, for back I cannot go.   220
BEATRICE [aside].
   Not this serpent gone yet?
VERMANDERO.   Look, girl, thy glove's fall'n;
   Stay, stay, De Flores, help a little.
DE FLORES.   Here, lady.
BEATRICE.
   Mischief on your officious forwardness;
   Who bade you stoop? They touch my hand no more;
   There, for t'other's sake I part with this;   225
   Take 'em and draw thine own skin off with 'em.
                   Exeunt [all but De Flores].
DE FLORES.
   Here's a favor come with a mischief now.
   I know she had rather wear my pelt tann'd
   In a pair of dancing pumps, than I should
   Thrust my fingers into her sockets here.   230
   I know she hates me, yet cannot choose but love her.
   No matter, if but to vex her, I'll haunt her still;
   Though I get nothing else, I'll have my will.   *Exit.*

[I.ii]   *Enter* Alibius *and* Lollio.

ALIBIUS.
   Lollio, I must trust thee with a secret,
   But thou must keep it.
LOLLIO.
   I was ever close to a secret, sir.
ALIBIUS.
   The diligence that I have found in thee,

227. mischief now.] *this edn.*; mischief: Now *Q*.

---

219. *murderers*] small cannon.

The care and industry already past,   5
Assures me of thy good continuance.
Lollio, I have a wife.

LOLLIO.

Fie, sir, 'tis too late to keep her secret; she's known to be
married all the town and country over.

ALIBIUS.

Thou goest too fast, my Lollio, that knowledge   10
I allow no man can be barr'd it;
But there is a knowledge which is nearer,
Deeper and sweeter, Lollio.

LOLLIO.

Well, sir, let us handle that between you and I.

ALIBIUS.

'Tis that I go about, man; Lollio,   15
My wife is young.

LOLLIO.

So much the worse to be kept secret, sir.

ALIBIUS.

Why, now thou meet'st the substance of the point;
I am old, Lollio.

LOLLIO.

No, sir, 'tis I am old Lollio.   20

ALIBIUS.

Yet why may not this concord and sympathize?
Old trees and young plants often grow together,
Well enough agreeing.

LOLLIO.

Ay, sir, but the old trees raise themselves higher and broader
than the young plants.   25

ALIBIUS.

Shrewd application. There's the fear, man;
I would wear my ring on my own finger;
Whilst it is borrowed it is none of mine
But his that useth it.

24–26. *old trees . . . application*] "The 'shrewd application' meant is, I
conceive, to that perpetual jest of the age, the cuckold's horns; which
Lollio supposes might raise Alibius's head above his wife's" (Dilke).

27. *I would . . . finger*] i.e., keep my wife to myself; cf. *Merchant of Venice*,
V.i.306–307.

LOLLIO.

You must keep it on still then; if it but lie by, one or other   30
will be thrusting into't.

ALIBIUS.

Thou conceiv'st me, Lollio; here thy watchful eye
Must have employment; I cannot always
Be at home.

LOLLIO.

I dare swear you cannot.   35

ALIBIUS.

I must look out.

LOLLIO.

I know't; you must look out, 'tis every man's case.

ALIBIUS.

Here I do say must thy employment be
To watch her treadings and in my absence
Supply my place.   40

LOLLIO.

I'll do my best, sir; yet surely I cannot see who you should
have cause to be jealous of.

ALIBIUS.

Thy reason for that, Lollio? 'Tis a comfortable question.

LOLLIO.

We have but two sorts of people in the house and both under
the whip, that's fools and madmen; the one has not wit   45
enough to be knaves and the other not knavery enough to be
fools.

ALIBIUS.

Ay, those are all my patients, Lollio.
I do profess the cure of either sort;
My trade, my living 'tis, I thrive by it.   50
But here's the care that mixes with my thrift:
The daily visitants that come to see
My brainsick patients I would not have
To see my wife. Gallants I do observe

---

52. *daily visitants*] The custom of visiting madhouses as places of entertainment was common in the seventeenth century. It is interesting to
observe that Isabella's advanced humanitarianism is not amused by the
spectacle (III.iii.43–44). See also the note at III.iii.18.

Of quick, enticing eyes, rich in habits,   55
Of stature and proportion very comely:
These are most shrewd temptations, Lollio.

LOLLIO.

They may be easily answered, sir. If they come to see the
fools and madmen, you and I may serve the turn, and let my
mistress alone; she's of neither sort.   60

ALIBIUS.

'Tis a good ward. Indeed come they to see
Our madmen or our fools; let 'em see no more
Than what they come for. By that consequent
They must not see her; I'm sure she's no fool.

LOLLIO.

And I'm sure she's no madman.   65

ALIBIUS.

Hold that buckler fast, Lollio; my trust
Is on thee, and I account it firm and strong.
What hour is't, Lollio?

LOLLIO.

Towards belly hour, sir.

ALIBIUS.

Dinner time? Thou mean'st twelve o'clock.   70

LOLLIO.

Yes, sir, for every part has his hour. We wake at six and look
about us, that's eye hour; at seven we should pray, that's knee
hour; at eight walk, that's leg hour; at nine gather flowers
and pluck a rose, that's nose hour; at ten we drink, that's
mouth hour; at eleven lay about us for victuals, that's hand   75
hour; at twelve go to dinner, that's belly hour.

ALIBIUS.

Profoundly, Lollio; it will be long
Ere all thy scholars learn this lesson, and
I did look to have a new one enter'd. Stay,
I think my expectation is come home.   80

Enter Pedro *and* Antonio [*dressed*] *like an Idiot.*

---

61. *ward*] guard (a fencing term).
66. *buckler*] shield.
74. *pluck a rose*] i.e., eliminate.

PEDRO.

Save you, sir, my business speaks itself;
This sight takes off the labor of my tongue.

ALIBIUS.

Ay, ay, sir, 'tis plain enough, you mean him
For my patient.

PEDRO.

And if your pains prove but commodious, to give but some   85
little strength to his sick and weak part of nature in him, these
are [*gives money*] but patterns to show you of the whole
pieces that will follow to you, beside the charge of diet, wash-
ing and other necessaries fully defrayed.

ALIBIUS.

Believe it, sir, there shall no care be wanting.   90

LOLLIO.

Sir, an officer in this place may deserve something; the
trouble will pass through my hands.

PEDRO.

'Tis fit something should come to your hands then, sir.

[*Gives money.*]

LOLLIO.

Yes, sir, 'tis I must keep him sweet and read to him. What
is his name?   95

PEDRO.

His name is Antonio; marry, we use but half to him,
only Tony.

LOLLIO.

Tony, Tony, 'tis enough and a very good name for a fool.
What's your name, Tony?

ANTONIO.

He, he, he, well, I thank you, cousin, he, he, he.   100

LOLLIO.

Good boy, hold up your head. He can laugh; I perceive by
that he is no beast.

PEDRO.

Well, sir,

---

85. *commodious*] beneficial medically.
101–102. *laugh . . . beast*] It was an Aristotelian commonplace that men
were distinguished from beasts by the ability to laugh.

If you can raise him but to any height,
Any degree of wit, might he attain,　　　　　　　105
As I might say, to creep but on all four
Towards the chair of wit or walk on crutches,
'Twould add an honor to your worthy pains,
And a great family might pray for you
To which he should be heir had he discretion　　　110
To claim and guide his own. Assure you, sir,
He is a gentleman.

LOLLIO.

Nay, there's nobody doubted that; at first sight I knew him
for a gentleman, he looks no other yet.

PEDRO.

Let him have good attendance and sweet lodging.　　115

LOLLIO.

As good as my mistress lies in, sir, and as you allow us time
and means, we can raise him to the higher degree of discretion.

PEDRO.

Nay, there shall no cost want, sir.

LOLLIO.

He will hardly be stretch'd up to the wit of a magnifico.

PEDRO.

Oh, no, that's not to be expected; far shorter will be enough.　120

LOLLIO.

I warrant you I'll make him fit to bear office in five weeks;
I'll undertake to wind him up to the wit of constable.

PEDRO.

If it be lower than that, it might serve turn.

LOLLIO.

No, fie, to level him with a headborough, beadle, or watchman, were but little better than he is; constable I'll able him.　125

121. I . . . I'll] *this edn.*; Ile warrant
you *Q. See Appendix A.*

---

118. *no cost want*] i.e., all of your expenses will be repaid.
119. *magnifico*] person of high judicial authority.
122. *wit of constable*] a proverbial expression for a very little intelligence;
cf. the constables in *Much Ado About Nothing.*
124. *headborough*] lowest parochial authority.
124. *beadle*] lowest judicial authority.
124–125. *watchman*] lowest civil authority.
125. *able him*] enable him to be.

If he do come to be a justice afterwards, let him thank the
keeper. Or I'll go further with you; say I do bring him up
to my own pitch, say I make him as wise as myself.

PEDRO.

Why, there I would have it.

LOLLIO.

Well, go to, either I'll be as arrant a fool as he, or he shall 130
be as wise as I, and then I think 'twill serve his turn.

PEDRO.

Nay, I do like thy wit passing well.

LOLLIO.

Yes, you may; yet if I had not been a fool, I had had more
wit than I have too; remember what state you find me in.

PEDRO.

I will, and so leave you; your best cares, I beseech you.   135

ALIBIUS.

Take you none with you; leave 'em all with us.   *Exit* Pedro.

ANTONIO.

Oh, my cousin's gone, cousin, cousin, oh!

LOLLIO.

Peace, peace, Tony, you must not cry, child; you must be
whipp'd if you do; your cousin is here still, I am your cousin,
Tony.   140

ANTONIO.

He, he, then I'll not cry, if thou be'st my cousin, he, he, he.

LOLLIO.

I were best try his wit a little, that I may know what form
to place him in.

ALIBIUS.

Ay, do, Lollio, do.

LOLLIO.

I must ask him easy questions at first. Tony, how many true 145
fingers has a tailor on his right hand?

---

136. S.D.] *after l. 134 in Q.*

---

134. *state*] professional position.
142. *try*] test.
142. *form*] class.
145–149. *true . . . deuce*] As all tailors were regarded as dishonest, the
answer is none—two less than two.

ANTONIO.

As many as on his left, cousin.

LOLLIO.

Good, and how many on both?

ANTONIO.

Two less than a deuce, cousin.

LOLLIO.

Very well answered. I come to you again, cousin Tony: how   150
many fools goes to a wise man?

ANTONIO.

Forty in a day sometimes, cousin.

LOLLIO.

Forty in a day? How prove you that?

ANTONIO.

All that fall out amongst themselves, and go to a lawyer to
be made friends.   155

LOLLIO.

A parlous fool, he must sit in the fourth form at least, I
perceive that. I come again, Tony: how many knaves make
an honest man?

ANTONIO.

I know not that, cousin.

LOLLIO.

No, the question is too hard for you; I'll tell you, cousin.   160
There's three knaves may make an honest man: a sergeant,
a jailer, and a beadle: the sergeant catches him, the jailor
holds him, and the beadle lashes him; and if he be not honest
then, the hangman must cure him.

ANTONIO.

Ha, ha, ha, that's fine sport, cousin.   165

ALIBIUS.

This was too deep a question for the fool, Lollio.

LOLLIO.

Yes, this might have serv'd yourself, though I say't. Once
more and you shall go play, Tony.

---

151. *goes to*] (1) make up—as Lollio means it; (2) visit—as Antonio
takes it.

ANTONIO.

Ay, play at push-pin, cousin, ha, he.

LOLLIO.

So thou shalt; say how many fools are here?   170

ANTONIO.

Two, cousin, thou and I.

LOLLIO.

Nay, y'are too forward there, Tony; mark my question: how
many fools and knaves are here: a fool before a knave, a fool
behind a knave, between every two fools a knave; how many
fools, how many knaves?   175

ANTONIO.

I never learnt so far, cousin.

ALIBIUS.

Thou putt'st too hard questions to him, Lollio.

LOLLIO.

I'll make him understand it easily; cousin, stand there.

ANTONIO.

Ay, cousin.

LOLLIO.

Master, stand you next the fool.   180

ALIBIUS.

Well, Lollio.

LOLLIO.

Here's my place. Mark now, Tony; there a fool before a
knave.

ANTONIO.

That's I, cousin.

LOLLIO.

Here's a fool behind a knave, that's I; and between us two   185
fools there is a knave, that's my master; 'tis but we three,
that's all.

ANTONIO.

We three, we three, cousin.

188.] Q adds on this line the S.D.:
"Mad-men within."

---

169. *push-pin*] a child's game, though, in view of Antonio's erotic purpose
in his disguise, suggestive of a more serious game.

186, 188. *we three*] alluding to the old sign of two idiots' heads with the
inscription "we three" (Dilke).

FIRST MADMAN (*within*).

Put's head i'th' pillory, the bread's too little.

SECOND MADMAN (*within*).

Fly, fly, and he catches the swallow.   190

THIRD MADMAN (*within*).

Give her more onion, or the devil put the rope about her crag.

LOLLIO.

You may hear what time of day it is, the chimes of Bedlam goes.

ALIBIUS.

Peace, peace, or the wire comes.

THIRD MADMAN (*within*).

Cat whore, cat whore, her parmesan, her parmesan.

ALIBIUS.

Peace, I say.—Their hour's come, they must be fed,   195
Lollio.

LOLLIO.

There's no hope of recovery of that Welsh madman; was
undone by a mouse that spoil'd him a parmesan; lost his
wits for't.

ALIBIUS.

Go to your charge, Lollio; I'll to mine.   200

LOLLIO.

Go you to your madmen's ward; let me alone with your fools.

ALIBIUS.

And remember my last charge, Lollio.

LOLLIO.

Of which your patients do you think I am?   *Exit* [Alibius].
—Come, Tony, you must amongst your schoolfellows now;
there's pretty scholars amongst 'em, I can tell you; there's   205
some of 'em at *stultus, stulta, stultum.*

ANTONIO.

I would see the madmen, cousin, if they would not bite me.

203. S.D.] *after l.* 202 *in* Q.

---

191. *crag*] neck.
192. *Bedlam*] a madhouse; originally, specifically, the asylum of St. Mary
of Bethlehem, just outside London.
193. *wire*] whip.
197. *Welsh madman*] In Jacobean times the Welsh were considered to be
inordinately fond of cheese.
206. *stultus . . . stultum*] the nominative singular of the three genders of
the Latin adjective "foolish."

LOLLIO.

    No, they shall not bite thee, Tony.

ANTONIO.

    They bite when they are at dinner, do they not, coz?

LOLLIO.

    They bite at dinner, indeed, Tony. Well, I hope to get credit 210
    by thee; I like thee the best of all the scholars that ever I
    brought up, and thou shalt prove a wise man, or I'll prove a
    fool myself.   *Exeunt.*

[II.i]   *Enter* Beatrice *and* Jasperino *severally.*

BEATRICE.

    Oh, sir, I'm ready now for that fair service
    Which makes the name of friend sit glorious on you.
    Good angels and this conduct be your guide;
    Fitness of time and place is there set down, sir.

JASPERINO.

    The joy I shall return rewards my service.   *Exit.* 5

BEATRICE.

    How wise is Alsemero in his friend!
    It is a sign he makes his choice with judgment.
    Then I appear in nothing more approv'd
    Than making choice of him;
    For 'tis a principle, he that can choose   10
    That bosom well, who of his thoughts partakes,
    Proves most discreet in every choice he makes.
    Methinks I love now with the eyes of judgment
    And see the way to merit, clearly see it.
    A true deserver like a diamond sparkles;   15
    In darkness you may see him, that's in absence,
    Which is the greatest darkness falls on love;
    Yet is he best discern'd then
    With intellectual eyesight. What's Piracquo
    My father spends his breath for? And his blessing   20
    Is only mine as I regard his name;

[II.i]

20–23. *his blessing . . . curse*] i.e., her father's blessing on her marriage is
given to her only if she regards his will and direction, otherwise it becomes
a curse.

Else it goes from me and turns head against me,
Transform'd into a curse. Some speedy way
Must be remember'd; he's so forward too,
So urgent that way, scarce allows me breath   25
To speak to my new comforts.

Enter De Flores.

DE FLORES [aside].   Yonder's she.
Whatever ails me? Now a-late especially
I can as well be hang'd as refrain seeing her;
Some twenty times a day, nay, not so little,
Do I force errands, frame ways and excuses   30
To come into her sight, and I have small reason for't
And less encouragement; for she baits me still
Every time worse than other, does profess herself
The cruelest enemy to my face in town,
At no hand can abide the sight of me,   35
As if danger, or ill-luck, hung in my looks.
I must confess, my face is bad enough,
But I know far worse has better fortune,
And not endur'd alone, but doted on.
And yet, such pick-hair'd faces, chins like witches',   40
Here and there five hairs whispering in a corner
As if they grew in fear one of another,
Wrinkles like troughs where swine deformity swills
The tears of perjury that lie there like wash
Fallen from the slimy and dishonest eye,   45
Yet such a one plucks sweets without restraint
And has the grace of beauty to his sweet.
Though my hard fate has thrust me out to servitude,
I tumbled into th' world a gentleman.

46. plucks] Dilke; pluckt Q.

---

32. baits] taunts.
35. At no hand] On no account.
40. pick-hair'd] "with hard, bristly hair and beard" (Bawcutt).
44. wash] medicinal lotion, here (as often) for the eyes.
47. has . . . sweet] enjoys in addition to the sweet (that he plucks) the satisfaction (1) of her being a beauty, (2) of her considering him a beautiful person. The metaphor is from dining: "grace" = blessing before eating; "sweet" = the tasty dessert that is eaten.

She turns her blessed eye upon me now,   50
And I'll endure all storms before I part with't.

BEATRICE.

Again!—

[*Aside*.]   This ominous ill-fac'd fellow more disturbs me
Than all my other passions.

DE FLORES [*aside*].   Now't begins again;
I'll stand this storm of hail though the stones pelt me.   55

BEATRICE.

Thy business? What's thy business?

DE FLORES [*aside*].   Soft and fair,
I cannot part so soon now.

BEATRICE [*aside*].   The villain's fix'd.—
Thou standing toad-pool.

DE FLORES [*aside*].   The shower falls amain now.

BEATRICE.

Who sent thee? What's thy errand? Leave my sight.

DE FLORES.

My lord your father charg'd me to deliver   60
A message to you.

BEATRICE.   What, another since?
Do't and be hang'd then; let me be rid of thee.

DE FLORES.

True service merits mercy.

BEATRICE.   What's thy message?

DE FLORES.

Let beauty settle but in patience,
You shall hear all.

BEATRICE.   A dallying, trifling torment.   65

DE FLORES.

Signor Alonzo de Piracquo, lady,
Sole brother to Tomazo de Piracquo—

BEATRICE.

Slave, when wilt make an end?

DE FLORES.   Too soon I shall.

68. wilt] *Dilke*; wil't Q.

---

58. *standing toad-pool*] stagnant and foul water, exuding toads and veno-
mous creatures.

BEATRICE.
    What all this while of him?
DE FLORES.   The said Alonzo
    With the foresaid Tomazo—
BEATRICE.   Yet again?   70
DE FLORES.
    Is new alighted.
BEATRICE.   Vengeance strike the news!
    Thou thing most loath'd, what cause was there in this
    To bring thee to my sight?
DE FLORES.   My lord your father
    Charg'd me to seek you out.
BEATRICE.   Is there no other
    To send his errand by?
DE FLORES.   It seems 'tis my luck   75
    To be i'th' way still.
BEATRICE.   Get thee from me.
DE FLORES.   So—
    [*Aside.*]   Why am not I an ass to devise ways
    Thus to be rail'd at? I must see her still;
    I shall have a mad qualm within this hour again,
    I know't, and like a common Garden bull   80
    I do but take breath to be lugg'd again.
    What this may bode I know not; I'll despair the less
    Because there's daily precedents of bad faces
    Belov'd beyond all reason. These foul chops
    May come into favor one day 'mongst his fellows.   85
    Wrangling has prov'd the mistress of good pastime;
    As children cry themselves asleep, I ha' seen
    Women have chid themselves abed to men.   *Exit* De Flores.
BEATRICE.
    I never see this fellow but I think
    Of some harm towards me; danger's in my mind still,   90
    I scarce leave trembling of an hour after.
    The next good mood I find my father in

---

80. *bull*] one of the ordinary bulls at the Paris Garden, an arena in Southwark for bull-baiting.
81. *lugg'd*] pulled by the hair or ears; baited.
85. *his*] i.e., their.

I'll get him quite discarded. Oh, I was
Lost in this small disturbance and forgot
Affliction's fiercer torrent that now comes   95
To bear down all my comforts.

Enter Vermandero, Alonzo, Tomazo.

VERMANDERO.   Y'are both welcome,
But an especial one belongs to you, sir,
To whose most noble name our love presents
The addition of a son, our son Alonzo.

ALONZO.
The treasury of honor cannot bring forth   100
A title I should more rejoice in, sir.

VERMANDERO.
You have improv'd it well. Daughter, prepare;
The day will steal upon thee suddenly.

BEATRICE [*aside*].
Howe'er, I will be sure to keep the night,
If it should come so near me.

[Beatrice *and* Vermandero *talk apart.*]

TOMAZO.   Alonzo.
ALONZO.   Brother.   105
TOMAZO.
In troth I see small welcome in her eye.

ALONZO.
Fie, you are too severe a censurer;
Of love in all points, there's no bringing on you;
If lovers should mark everything a fault,
Affection would be like an ill-set book   110
Whose faults might prove as big as half the volume.

107. censurer;] *this edn.*; censurer   108. you;] *Dilke*; you *Q.*
Q.

---

100. *treasury of honor*] dignity of honorific titles.
104. *keep the night*] (1) be on the alert during the bridal night; (2) retain
control and protection of myself during the night.
108. *there's ... you*] "I cannot bring you to a more reasonable point of
view" (Bawcutt).
111. *faults*] list of errata.

BEATRICE.

That's all I do entreat.

VERMANDERO.　　　　　　It is but reasonable;

I'll see what my son says to't. —Son Alonzo,

Here's a motion made but to reprieve

A maidenhead three days longer; the request　　　　　115

Is not far out of reason, for indeed

The former time is pinching.

ALONZO.　　　　　　　Though my joys

Be set back so much time as I could wish

They had been forward, yet since she desires it,

The time is set as pleasing as before,　　　　　120

I find no gladness wanting.

VERMANDERO.　　　　　May I ever

Meet it in that point still. Y'are nobly welcome, sirs.

　　　　　　　　　　　Exeunt Vermandero *and* Beatrice.

TOMAZO.

So, did you mark the dullness of her parting now?

ALONZO.

What dullness? Thou art so exceptious still.

TOMAZO.

Why, let it go then; I am but a fool　　　　　125

To mark your harms so heedfully.

ALONZO.　　　　　　　　Where's the oversight?

TOMAZO.

Come, your faith's cozened in her, strongly cozened.

Unsettle your affection with all speed

Wisdom can bring it to, your peace is ruin'd else.

Think what a torment 'tis to marry one　　　　　130

Whose heart is leap'd into another's bosom:

If ever pleasure she receive from thee,

It comes not in thy name or of thy gift;

She lies but with another in thine arms,

He the half father unto all thy children;　　　　　135

In the conception, if he get 'em not,

She helps to get 'em for him; and how dangerous

137. him; and] *Dilke*; him, in his
passions, and *Q*.

---

127. *cozened*] cheated.

And shameful her restraint may go in time to,
It is not to be thought on without sufferings.

ALONZO.
You speak as if she lov'd some other then.   140

TOMAZO.
Do you apprehend so slowly?

ALONZO.   Nay, and that
Be your fear only, I am safe enough.
Preserve your friendship and your counsel, brother,
For times of more distress. I should depart
An enemy, a dangerous, deadly one   145
To any but thyself that should but think
She knew the meaning of inconstancy
Much less the use and practice; yet w'are friends.
Pray let no more be urg'd; I can endure
Much till I meet an injury to her,   150
Then I am not myself. Farewell, sweet brother,
How much w'are bound to heaven to depart lovingly.
                                                             Exit.

TOMAZO.
Why here is love's tame madness; thus a man
Quickly steals into his vexation.   *Exit.*

[II.ii]   *Enter* Diaphanta *and* Alsemero.

DIAPHANTA.
The place is my charge, you have kept your hour,
And the reward of a just meeting bless you.
I hear my lady coming; complete gentleman,
I dare not be too busy with my praises,

148. w'are]   Q   (*corr.*);   we   are
Q (*uncorr.*).

---

138. *her . . . to*] the effects of excessively restraining her may become in
the future.
[II.ii]
    1. *place*] presumably the concealed route ("private way") through which
Diaphanta has led the lover, or an antechamber to the bedroom under her
supervision.
    3. *complete*] i.e., "perfect."
    4. *praises*] i.e., of you.

Th'are dangerous things to deal with.   *Exit.*

ALSEMERO.   This goes well;   5
    These women are the ladies' cabinets;
    Things of most precious trust are lock'd into 'em.

                 Enter Beatrice.

BEATRICE.
    I have within mine eye all my desires;
    Requests that holy prayers ascend heaven for
    And brings 'em down to furnish our defects   10
    Come not more sweet to our necessities
    Than thou unto my wishes.

ALSEMERO.   W'are so like
    In our expressions, lady, that unless I borrow
    The same words, I shall never find their equals.

BEATRICE.
    How happy were this meeting, this embrace,   15
    If it were free from envy? This poor kiss,
    It has an enemy, a hateful one
    That wishes poison to't. How well were I now
    If there were none such name known as Piracquo?
    Nor no such tie as the command of parents?   20
    I should be but too much blessed.

ALSEMERO.   One good service
    Would strike off both your fears, and I'll go near it too
    Since you are so distress'd. Remove the cause,
    The command ceases; so there's two fears blown out
    With one and the same blast.

BEATRICE.   Pray let me find you, sir;   25
    What might that service be so strangely happy?

ALSEMERO.
    The honorablest piece 'bout man, valor.
    I'll send a challenge to Piracquo instantly.

7. lock'd] *Dilke*; lock *Q*.

    9–10. *Requests . . . defects*] Prayers that carry requests to heaven and
bring back the providential gifts to supply our needs.
    23–24. *cause . . . command*] i.e., the cause is Piracquo; the command is
her father's order.
    25. *let . . . you*] i.e., "you've lost me"; I do not understand.

BEATRICE.

How? Call you that extinguishing of fear
When 'tis the only way to keep it flaming?   30
Are not you ventured in the action
That's all my joys and comforts? Pray, no more, sir.
Say you prevail'd; you're danger's and not mine then.
The law would claim you from me, or obscurity
Be made the grave to bury you alive.   35
I'm glad these thoughts come forth; oh, keep not one
Of this condition, sir. Here was a course
Found to bring sorrow on her way to death;
The tears would ne'er 'a' dried till dust had chok'd 'em.
Blood-guiltiness becomes a fouler visage,   40
And now I think on one—[*Aside.*]   I was too blame,
I ha' marr'd so good a market with my scorn;
'T had been done questionless. The ugliest creature
Creation fram'd for some use, yet to see
I could not mark so much where it should be.   45

ALSEMERO.

Lady.

BEATRICE [*aside*]. Why, men of art make much of poison,
Keep one to expel another; where was my art?

ALSEMERO.

Lady, you hear not me.

BEATRICE.   I do especially, sir;
The present times are not so sure of our side
As those hereafter may be; we must use 'em then   50
As thrifty folks their wealth, sparingly now
Till the time opens.

ALSEMERO.   You teach wisdom, lady.

BEATRICE.

Within there, Diaphanta.

33. you're] *Dyce*; your *Q*.

41–42. *too blame . . . scorn*] too blameworthy in that I might have spoiled
my own chances to purchase at a market (De Flores) a commodity (murder)
that I now need. See Appendix A.

44. *for some use*] The doctrine that everything in creation is serviceable
is traditional; see Middleton's *Women Beware Women*, I.ii.44–49.

52. *opens*] becomes auspicious.

−31−

Enter Diaphanta.

DIAPHANTA.   Do you call, madam?
BEATRICE.
Perfect your service and conduct this gentleman
The private way you brought him.
DIAPHANTA.   I shall, madam.   55
ALSEMERO.
My love's as firm as love e'er built upon.

Exeunt Diaphanta *and* Alsemero.

Enter De Flores.

DE FLORES [*aside*].
I have watch'd this meeting and do wonder much
What shall become of t'other; I'm sure both
Cannot be serv'd unless she trangress. Happily
Then I'll put in for one; for if a woman   60
Fly from one point, from him she makes a husband,
She spreads and mounts then like arithmetic,
One, ten, one hundred, one thousand, ten thousand,
Proves in time sutler to an army royal.
Now do I look to be most richly rail'd at,   65
Yet I must see her.
BEATRICE [*aside*].   Why, put case I loath'd him
As much as youth and beauty hates a sepulcher,
Must I needs show it? Cannot I keep that secret
And serve my turn upon him? See, he's here.—
De Flores.
DE FLORES [*aside*]. Ha, I shall run mad with joy;   70
She call'd me fairly by my name De Flores
And neither rogue nor rascal.
BEATRICE.   What ha' you done
To your face a-late? Y'ave met with some good physician;
Y'ave prun'd yourself, methinks; you were not wont

---

64. *sutler*] camp-follower engaged in selling supplies to the soldiers.
64. *army royal*] particularly large military force, army on a grand scale
(*OED*, "royal," 10.b).
69. *serve . . . him*] use him for my own purpose.
74. *prun'd*] preened.

To look so amorously.

DE FLORES [*aside*].   Not I,   75
'Tis the same physnomy to a hair and pimple
Which she call'd scurvy scarce an hour ago.
How is this?

BEATRICE.   Come hither; nearer, man.

DE FLORES [*aside*].
I'm up to the chin in heaven.

BEATRICE.   Turn, let me see;
Faugh, 'tis but the heat of the liver, I perceiv't.   80
I thought it had been worse.

DE FLORES [*aside*].   Her fingers touch'd me;
She smells all amber.

BEATRICE.
I'll make a water for you shall cleanse this
Within a fortnight.

DE FLORES.   With your own hands, lady?

BEATRICE.
Yes, mine own, sir; in a work of cure,   85
I'll trust no other.

DE FLORES [*aside*].   'Tis half an act of pleasure
To hear her talk thus to me.

BEATRICE.   When w'are us'd
To a hard face, 'tis not so unpleasing.
It mends still in opinion, hourly mends,
I see it by experience.

DE FLORES [*aside*].   I was blest   90
To light upon this minute; I'll make use on't.

BEATRICE.
Hardness becomes the visage of a man well;
It argues service, resolution, manhood,
If cause were of employment.

DE FLORES.   'Twould be soon seen
If e'er your ladyship had cause to use it.   95

---

75. *amorously*] "like a lover" (Spencer).

76. *physnomy*] physiognomy.

80. *heat . . . liver*] The liver was traditionally one of the seats of love and
violent passions; Beatrice's speech is ironically truer than she supposes.

82. *amber*] sweetly perfumed with ambergris.

83. *water*] i.e., a wash, as at II.i.44.

I would but wish the honor of a service
So happy as that mounts to.
BEATRICE.   We shall try you.
Oh, my De Flores!
DE FLORES [aside].   How's that?
She calls me hers already, "my De Flores."—
You were about to sigh out somewhat, madam.   100
BEATRICE.
No, was I? I forgot. Oh!
DE FLORES.   There 'tis again,
The very fellow on't.
BEATRICE.   You are too quick, sir.
DE FLORES.
There's no excuse for't now, I heard it twice, madam.
That sigh would fain have utterance; take pity on't
And lend it a free word; 'las, how it labors   105
For liberty, I hear the murmur yet
Beat at your bosom.
BEATRICE.   Would creation—
DE FLORES.
Ay, well said, that's it.
BEATRICE.   Had form'd me man.
DE FLORES.
Nay, that's not it.
BEATRICE.   Oh, 'tis the soul of freedom;
I should not then be forc'd to marry one   110
I hate beyond all depths; I should have power
Then to oppose my loathings, nay, remove 'em
Forever from my sight.
DE FLORES.   Oh, blest occasion!
Without change to your sex you have your wishes.
Claim so much man in me.
BEATRICE.   In thee, De Flores?   115
There's small cause for that.
DE FLORES.   Put it not from me,
It's a service that I kneel for to you.   [Kneels.]
BEATRICE.
You are too violent to mean faithfully;
There's horror in my service, blood, and danger;

–34–

Can those be things to sue for?

DE FLORES.   If you knew   120
How sweet it were to me to be employed
In any act of yours, you would say then
I fail'd and us'd not reverence enough
When I receive the charge on't.

BEATRICE [aside].   This is much, methinks;
Belike his wants are greedy, and to such   125
Gold tastes like angels' food. —Rise.

DE FLORES.
I'll have the work first.

BEATRICE [aside].   Possible his need
Is strong upon him. —There's to encourage thee;

                                   [Gives money.]

As thou art forward and thy service dangerous,
Thy reward shall be precious.

DE FLORES.   That I have thought on;   130
I have assur'd myself of that beforehand
And know it will be precious; the thought ravishes.

BEATRICE.
Then take him to thy fury.

DE FLORES.   I thirst for him.

BEATRICE.
Alonzo de Piracquo.

DE FLORES.
His end's upon him; he shall be seen no more.   [Rises.]   135

BEATRICE.
How lovely now dost thou appear to me!
Never was man dearlier rewarded.

DE FLORES.
I do think of that.

131. myself of that] Q (corr.);
my selfe that Q (uncorr.).

_____

126. angels' food] An extreme parallel. In Christian tradition, angels'
food is the bread of heaven (panis angelorum), consubstantial with the manna
of the Old Testament and the body of Christ in the New (see Aquinas,
"Lauda Sion Salvatorem").

129. As . . . forward] In proportion as thou art bold and active in this
deed.

BEATRICE.
> Be wondrous careful in the execution.

DE FLORES.
> Why, are not both our lives upon the cast?   140

BEATRICE.
> Then I throw all my fears upon thy service.

DE FLORES.
> They ne'er shall rise to hurt you.   When the deed's done,
> I'll furnish thee with all things for thy flight;
> Thou may'st live bravely in another country.

DE FLORES.
> Ay, ay, we'll talk of that hereafter.   145

BEATRICE [aside].
> I shall rid myself of two inveterate loathings
> At one time: Piracquo and his dog-face.   *Exit.*

DE FLORES.
> Oh, my blood!
> Methinks I feel her in mine arms already,
> Her wanton fingers combing out this beard   150
> And, being pleased, praising this bad face;
> Hunger and pleasure, they'll commend sometimes
> Slovenly dishes and feed heartily on 'em;
> Nay, which is stranger, refuse daintier for 'em.
> Some women are odd feeders. I'm too loud.   155
> Here comes the man goes supperless to bed,
> Yet shall not rise tomorrow to his dinner.

Enter Alonzo.

ALONZO.
> De Flores.

DE FLORES.   My kind, honorable lord.

ALONZO.
> I am glad I ha' met with thee.

DE FLORES.   Sir.

ALONZO.
> Thou canst show me the full strength of the castle?   160

DE FLORES.
> That I can, sir.

---

147. *his dog-face*] a construction on the pattern of "his lordship."

ALONZO.   I much desire it.

DE FLORES.

And if the ways and straits of some of the
Passages be not too tedious for you,
I will assure you worth your time and sight,
My lord.

ALONZO.   Puh, that shall be no hindrance.   165

DE FLORES.

I'm your servant, then. 'Tis now near dinner time;
'Gainst your lordship's rising I'll have the keys
About me.

ALONZO.   Thanks, kind De Flores.

DE FLORES [aside].

He's safely thrust upon me beyond hopes.   *Exeunt.*

(*In the act-time,* De Flores *hides a naked rapier.*)

[III.i, ii]   *Enter* Alonzo *and* De Flores.

DE FLORES.

Yes, here are all the keys; I was afraid, my lord,   [i.l]
I'd wanted for the postern: this is it.
I've all, I've all, my lord; this for the sconce.

ALONZO.

'Tis a most spacious and impregnable fort.

DE FLORES.

You'll tell me more, my lord. This descent   5
Is somewhat narrow; we shall never pass
Well with our weapons; they'll but trouble us.

ALONZO.

Thou say'st true.

DE FLORES.   Pray let me help your lordship.

ALONZO.

'Tis done. Thanks, kind De Flores.

DE FLORES.   Here are hooks, my lord,   *

169.1.] *Q places this S.D. after the
entry direction of III.i.*

---

167. *'Gainst . . . rising*] before you have risen from dinner.
169.1. *act-time*] interval between Acts II and III.
[III.i]
3. *sconce*] small fort.

To hang such things on purpose.

ALONZO.   Lead, I'll follow thee.   10

Exeunt at one door and enter at the other.

DE FLORES.

All this is nothing, you shall see anon   [ii.1]
A place you little dream on.

ALONZO.   I am glad
I have this leisure; all your master's house
Imagine I ha' taken a gondola.

DE FLORES.

All but myself, sir—[*aside*]   which makes up my safety.—   5
My lord, I'll place you at a casement here
Will show you the full strength of all the castle.
Look, spend your eye awhile upon that object.

ALONZO.

Here's rich variety, De Flores.

DE FLORES.   Yes, sir.

ALONZO.

Goodly munition.

DE FLORES.   Ay, there's ordnance, sir,   10
No bastard metal, will ring you a peal like bells
At great men's funerals. Keep your eye straight, my lord;
Take special notice of that sconce before you,
There you may dwell awhile.

ALONZO.   I am upon't.

DE FLORES.

And so am I.   [*Stabs him.*]

ALONZO.   De Flores, oh, De Flores,   15
Whose malice hast thou put on?

DE FLORES.   Do you question
A work of secrecy? I must silence you.   [*Stabs him.*]

ALONZO.

Oh, oh, oh.

DE FLORES.   I must silence you.   [*Stabs him; he dies.*]
So, here's an undertaking well accomplish'd.

[III.i]
   10.1. *Exeunt . . . other.*] The direction implies a change of location, but it
does not mark the beginning of a new scene, because neither the actors nor
the matters of the action change. In order to facilitate reference, however,
this edition follows the traditional scene division.

This vault serves to good use now. Ha! what's that   20
Threw sparkles in my eye? Oh, 'tis a diamond
He wears upon his finger; it was well found,
This will approve the work. What, so fast on?
Not part in death? I'll take a speedy course then;
Finger and all shall off. [*Cuts off finger.*] So, now I'll clear   25
The passages from all suspect or fear.   *Exit with body.*

[III.iii]   *Enter* Isabella *and* Lollio.

ISABELLA.

Why, sirrah? Whence have you commission
To fetter the doors against me? If you
Keep me in a cage, pray whistle to me,
Let me be doing something.

LOLLIO.

You shall be doing, if it please you; I'll whistle to you if you'll   5
pipe after.

ISABELLA.

Is it your master's pleasure or your own
To keep me in this pinfold?

LOLLIO.

'Tis for my master's pleasure, lest being taken in another
man's corn, you might be pounded in another place.   10

ISABELLA.

'Tis very well, and he'll prove very wise.

LOLLIO.

He says you have company enough in the house, if you please
to be sociable, of all sorts of people.

ISABELLA.

Of all sorts? Why, here's none but fools and madmen.

LOLLIO.

Very well; and where will you find any other, if you   15
should go abroad? There's my master and I to boot too.

[III.ii]
   23. *approve*] give proof of.
   26. *suspect*] suspicion.
[III.iii]
   8. *pinfold*] pen, or fold, for confining stray animals.
   10. *pounded*] (1) impounded; (2) pressed.

ISABELLA.

Of either sort one, a madman and a fool.

LOLLIO.

I would ev'n participate of both then if I were as you. I
know y'are half mad already; be half foolish too.

ISABELLA.

Y'are a brave saucy rascal. Come on, sir,   20
Afford me then the pleasure of your bedlam;
You were commending once today to me
Your last-come lunatic: what a proper
Body there was without brains to guide it,
And what a pitiful delight appear'd   25
In that defect, as if your wisdom had found
A mirth in madness. Pray, sir, let me partake
If there be such a pleasure.

LOLLIO.

If I do not show you the handsomest, discreetest madman,
one that I may call the understanding madman, then say I   30
am a fool.

ISABELLA.

Well, a match, I will say so.

LOLLIO.

When you have a taste of the madman, you shall, if you
please, see fools' college, o'th' side; I seldom lock there, 'tis
but shooting a bolt or two and you are amongst 'em. *Exit.* 35
[*Within.*]   Come on, sir, let me see how handsomely you'll
behave yourself now.

Enter Lollio [*and*] Franciscus.

FRANCISCUS.

How sweetly she looks! Oh, but there's a wrinkle in her

33. if you] Q (*corr.*); if yon Q   35. S.D. *Exit.*] *this edn.; Ex. Enter*
(*uncorr.*).   *presently. Q.*

---

18. *participate*] Lollio does not need the presence of another suitor (as at
ll. 214–242) to spur him to soliciting his mistress; his comments at ll. 5–6
and here disclose that he—not the daily visitant—is the man Alibius should
fear.

23. *proper*] handsome.

35. *shooting a bolt*] sliding back the bar that latches the door; with a
possible echo of the proverb "A fool's bolt is soon shot," though this has
reference to shooting a cross-bow and seems an irrelevant association here.

brow as deep as philosophy. Anacreon, drink to my mistress'
health, I'll pledge it. Stay, stay, there's a spider in the cup;   40
no, 'tis but a grapestone; swallow it, fear nothing, poet; so,
so, lift higher.

ISABELLA.

Alack, alack, 'tis too full of pity
To be laugh'd at. How fell he mad? Canst thou tell?

LOLLIO.

For love, mistress. He was a pretty poet too, and that set   45
him forwards first; the muses then forsook him, he ran mad
for a chambermaid, yet she was but a dwarf neither.

FRANCISCUS.

Hail, bright Titania,
Why stand'st thou idle on these flowery banks?
Oberon is dancing with his dryades;   50
I'll gather daisies, primrose, violets,
And bind them in a verse of poesie.

LOLLIO.

Not too near, you see your danger.   [Shows whip.]

FRANCISCUS.

Oh, hold thy hand, great Diomede;
Thou feed'st thy horses well, they shall obey thee.   55
Get up, Bucephalus kneels.   [Kneels.]

39–42. *Anacreon . . . higher*] An allusion to the legend of the poet Anacreon
who choked on a grapestone while drinking wine and died (Pliny, *Natural
History*, VII,7). The comforting assurance that the object is not a spider
(thought to be poisonous) but only a harmless grapestone is thus deceptive.

48, 50. *Titania, Oberon*] the queen and king of the fairies (as represented
in *A Midsummer Night's Dream*). "Franciscus insinuates that Oberon (i.e.,
Alibius) is out enjoying himself with other women ('dancing with his
dryades' [wood-nymphs]), and suggests that Titania (i.e., Isabella)
should solace herself with him" (Bawcutt).

54–55. *Diomede . . . thee*] either (1) the Greek hero, rewarded with the
Thracian horses of Rhesus for his exploit in capturing them in the *Iliad*,
Book X (Chapman, 1611, p. 141):

> . . . in the tent of *Diomed* they plac't
> The horse without contention, as his deservings meed;
> Which (with his other horse set up) on yellow wheat did feed.

(*horse* in both uses is plural); or (2) the king of the Bistonians in Thrace who
fed his horses with human flesh. Both sets of horses are discussed by Servius
in his Commentary on the *Aeneid*, Book I: the former at 1. 469, and both
at 1. 756.

56. *Get up*] i.e., on my back as if I were a horse.

56. *Bucephalus*] the fabulous horse of Alexander the Great.

LOLLIO.

You see how I awe my flock? A shepherd has not his dog at
more obedience.

ISABELLA.

His conscience is unquiet; sure that was
The cause of this. A proper gentleman.   60

FRANCISCUS.

Come hither, Aesculapius, hide the poison.

LOLLIO.

Well, 'tis hid.   [*Conceals whip.*]

FRANCISCUS.

Didst thou never hear of one Tiresias,
A famous poet?   [*Rises.*]

LOLLIO.

Yes, that kept tame wild-geese.   65

FRANCISCUS.

That's he; I am the man.

LOLLIO.

No.

FRANCISCUS.

Yes, but make no words on't; I was a man
Seven years ago.

LOLLIO.

A stripling, I think you might.   70

FRANCISCUS.

Now I'm a woman, all feminine.

LOLLIO.

I would I might see that.

FRANCISCUS.

Juno struck me blind.

LOLLIO.

I'll ne'er believe that; for a woman, they say, has an eye
more than a man.   75

---

61. *Aesculapius*] Greek god of medicine; Alibius and Lollio are charged
with the cure of the inmates.

63–76. *Tiresias . . . blind*] An allusion to the famous prophet (not poet)
who was changed from a man to a woman and seven years later was
changed back. Juno struck him blind for having decided against her in a
dispute with Jupiter.

FRANCISCUS.

I say she struck me blind.

LOLLIO.

And Luna made you mad; you have two trades to beg with.

FRANCISCUS.

Luna is now big-bellied, and there's room
For both of us to ride with Hecate.
I'll drag thee up into her silver sphere,   80
And there we'll kick the dog and beat the bush
That barks against the witches of the night;
The swift lycanthropi that walks the round
We'll tear their wolvish skins and save the sheep. [*Beats* Lollio.]

LOLLIO.

Is't come to this? Nay then, my poison comes forth again;   85
mad slave indeed, abuse your keeper?   [*Shows whip.*]

ISABELLA.

I prithee hence with him, now he grows dangerous.

FRANCISCUS (*sings*).

Sweet love, pity me;
Give me leave to lie with thee.

LOLLIO.

No, I'll see you wiser first. To your own kennel.   90

FRANCISCUS.

No noise, she sleeps, draw all the curtains round;
Let no soft sound molest the pretty soul
But love, and love creeps in at a mouse-hole.

LOLLIO.

I would you would get into your hole.   *Exit* Franciscus.
Now, mistress, I will bring you another sort; you shall be   95
fool'd another while. Tony, come hither, Tony.

88. S.P. *sings*] *Dilke*; *Sing.* Q.

---

77. *Luna . . . mad*] lunatics are made by Luna, the moon.

77. *two trades*] blindness and madness; for the begging madman cf. Edgar in *King Lear*.

78. *big-bellied*] (1) full; (2) pregnant.

79. *Hecate*] another name for the goddess of the moon.

81. *kick . . . bush*] probably nonsense, but "beat the bush" means "proceed deviously" (*Dict. of Slang*) and though "kick the dog" is unknown, "kick the cat" means "bustle about" in Nottinghamshire dialect (*Dialect Dict.*). The dog and the bush are traditional companions of the man in the moon (cf. *A Midsummer Night's Dream*, V.i.136–137).

83. *lycanthropi*] madmen under the delusion that they are wolves.

Enter Antonio.

Look who's yonder, Tony.

ANTONIO.

Cousin, is it not my aunt?

LOLLIO.

Yes, 'tis one of 'em, Tony.

ANTONIO.

He, he, how do you, uncle?　　　　　　　　　　　　　　100

LOLLIO.

Fear him not, mistress; 'tis a gentle nidget. You may play
with him, as safely with him as with his bauble.

ISABELLA.

How long hast thou been a fool?

ANTONIO.

Ever since I came hither, cousin.

ISABELLA.

Cousin? I'm none of thy cousins, fool.　　　　　　　　105

LOLLIO.

Oh, mistress, fools have always so much wit as to claim
their kindred.

MADMAN (*within*).

Bounce, bounce, he falls, he falls.

ISABELLA.

Hark you, your scholars in the upper room
Are out of order.　　　　　　　　　　　　　　　　　110

LOLLIO.

Must I come amongst you there? Keep you the fool,
mistress; I'll go up and play left-handed Orlando amongst
the madmen.　　　　　　　　　　　　　　　　*Exit.*

---

98. *aunt*] a slang term for a mistress or a bawd; cf. *The Winter's Tale*,
IV.ii.11.

101. *nidget*] idiot; a nidget = an idiot.

102. *bauble*] stick (often phallic in shape) carried by an idiot or fool;
references to it are usually indecent (cf. *Romeo and Juliet*, II.iv.97).

105. *Cousin*] "It is common in Elizabethan drama for an unfaithful woman
and her lover to gain access to each other by pretending to be cousins. . . .
This may help to account for Isabella's indignant repudiation of the
relationship" (Bawcutt).

112. *play . . . Orlando*] be a poor imitation of the great hero Orlando (in
Ariosto's *Orlando Furioso*).

ISABELLA.
  Well, sir.
ANTONIO.
  'Tis opportuneful now, sweet lady. Nay,   115
  Cast no amazing eye upon this change.
ISABELLA.
  Ha!
ANTONIO.
  This shape of folly shrouds your dearest love,
  The truest servant to your powerful beauties,
  Whose magic had this force thus to transform me.   120
ISABELLA.
  You are a fine fool, indeed.
ANTONIO.   Oh, 'tis not strange;
  Love has an intellect that runs through all
  The scrutinous sciences and, like
  A cunning poet, catches a quantity
  Of every knowledge; yet brings all home   125
  Into one mystery, into one secret
  That he proceeds in.
ISABELLA.   Y'are a parlous fool.
ANTONIO.
  No danger in me; I bring nought but love
  And his soft, wounding shafts to strike you with.
  Try but one arrow; if it hurt you,   130
  I'll stand you twenty back in recompense.
ISABELLA.
  A forward fool, too.
ANTONIO.   This was love's teaching;
  A thousand ways he fashion'd out my way,
  And this I found the safest and the nearest
  To tread the galaxia to my star.   135
ISABELLA.
  Profound withal. Certain, you dream'd of this;

133. he] *Dyce*; she *Q*.   134. the nearest] *Dilke*; neerest *Q*.

114–213. See Introduction, pp. xxi–xxiv, for comments on seduction, submission, and structure in this sequence.
127. *parlous*] (1) dangerously cunning; (2) perilous.
130. *arrow*] kiss (?).
135. *galaxia*] Milky Way.

–45–

Love never taught it waking.

ANTONIO.   Take no acquaintance
Of these outward follies; there is within
A gentleman that loves you.

ISABELLA.   When I see him,
I'll speak with him; so in the meantime   140
Keep your habit, it becomes you well enough.
As you are a gentleman, I'll not discover you;
That's all the favor that you must expect.
When you are weary, you may leave the school,
For all this while you have but play'd the fool.   145

Enter Lollio.

ANTONIO.
And must again. He, he, I thank you, cousin;
I'll be your valentine tomorrow morning.

LOLLIO.
How do you like the fool, mistress?

ISABELLA.
Passing well, sir.

LOLLIO.
Is he not witty, pretty well for a fool?   150

ISABELLA.
If he hold on as he begins, he is like
To come to something.

LOLLIO.
Ay, thank a good tutor. You may put him to't; he begins to
answer pretty hard questions. Tony, how many is five
times six?   155

ANTONIO.
Five times six is six times five.

LOLLIO.
What arithmetician could have answer'd better? How
many is one hundred and seven?

ANTONIO.
One hundred and seven is seven hundred and one, cousin.

LOLLIO.
This is no wit to speak on. Will you be rid of the fool now? 160

ISABELLA.
By no means; let him stay a little.

---

141. *habit*] clothing.

MADMEN (*within*).

Catch there, catch the last couple in hell.

LOLLIO.

Again? Must I come amongst you? Would my master were
come home! I am not able to govern both these wards
together.   *Exit.* 165

ANTONIO.

Why should a minute of love's hour be lost?

ISABELLA.

Fie, out again! I had rather you kept
Your other posture; you become not your tongue
When you speak from your clothes.

ANTONIO.   How can he freeze

Lives near so sweet a warmth? Shall I alone   170
Walk through the orchard of the Hesperides
And cowardly not dare to pull an apple?
This with the red cheeks I must venture for.

Enter Lollio *above.*

ISABELLA.

Take heed, there's giants keep 'em.   [Antonio *kisses her.*]

LOLLIO [*aside*].

How now, fool, are you good at that? Have you read 175
Lipsius? He's past *Ars Amandi*; I believe I must put harder
questions to him, I perceive that—

---

162. *Catch . . . hell*] A cry in the game of barley-break. The game was
played by three couples, hand in hand, those in a center circle, called "hell,"
attempting to catch the others as they ran past them from one end of the
court to the other. Sidney describes a complete course of the game in "A
Shepheards tale no height of stile desires" (*Works*, II [1922], 219–224).
See also V.iii.163–164.
169. *speak from*] speak in a manner not in keeping with.
171–172. *Walk . . . apple*] The orchard bore golden apples guarded by
the Hesperides and the hundred-headed dragon, Ladon, the offspring of
the giant Tython (see below, 1. 174).
173. *This*] i.e., This one. Some editors provide for a kiss at 1. 131, but
the present venture is surely the first; its success is confirmed by Lollio's
remarks.
176. *Lipsius*] "Is it necessary to notice that the name of this great scholar
is introduced merely for the sake of its first syllable?" (Dyce).
176. *Ars Amandi*] *The Art of Loving*, a treatise by Ovid, often cited to show
a gallant's proficiency.

ISABELLA.

You are bold without fear too.

ANTONIO.   What should I fear,
Having all joys about me? Do you smile
And love shall play the wanton on your lip,   180
Meet and retire, retire and meet again;
Look you but cheerfully, and in your eyes
I shall behold mine own deformity
And dress myself up fairer. I know this shape
Becomes me not, but in those bright mirrors   185
I shall array me handsomely.

LOLLIO [*aside*].

Cuckoo, cuckoo.   *Exit* [*above*]

[*Enter*] *Madmen above* [*and pass over*]; *some as birds, others as beasts.*

ANTONIO.

What are these?

ISABELLA.   Of fear enough to part us,
Yet are they but our schools of lunatics,
That act their fantasies in any shapes   190
Suiting their present thoughts; if sad, they cry;
If mirth be their conceit, they laugh again.
Sometimes they imitate the beasts and birds,
Singing or howling, braying, barking; all
As their wild fancies prompt 'em.

ANTONIO.   These are no fears.   195

Enter Lollio.

ISABELLA.

But here's a large one, my man.

ANTONIO.

Ha, he, that's fine sport indeed, cousin.

LOLLIO.

I would my master were come home; 'tis too much for one

---

187. *Cuckoo*] a premonition of cuckoldry.
187.1. There is no reason to suppose that the madmen are clothed as animals (they are certainly not wearing their costumes for the masque which Alibius has not yet announced); they "imitate the beasts and birds" by "singing or howling, braying, barking" (ll. 193–94).

shepherd to govern two of these flocks, nor can I believe that
one churchman can instruct two benefices at once; there   200
will be some incurable mad of the one side and very fools
on the other. Come, Tony.

ANTONIO.

Prithee cousin, let me stay here still.

LOLLIO.

No, you must to your book now, you have play'd sufficiently.

ISABELLA.

Your fool is grown wondrous witty.   205

LOLLIO.

Well, I'll say nothing, but I do not think but he will put
you down one of these days.   *Exeunt* Lollio *and* Antonio.

ISABELLA.

Here the restrained current might make breach,
Spite of the watchful bankers. Would a woman stray,
She need not gad abroad to seek her sin,   210
It would be brought home one ways or other;
The needle's point will to the fixed north,
Such drawing arctics women's beauties are.

Enter Lollio.

LOLLIO.

How dost thou, sweet rogue?

ISABELLA.

How now?   215

LOLLIO.

Come, there are degrees; one fool may be better than
another.

ISABELLA.

What's the matter?

LOLLIO.

Nay, if thou giv'st thy mind to fool's-flesh, have at thee.

ISABELLA.   [*Tries to kiss her.*]

You bold slave, you.   220

---

200. *one churchman . . . benefices*] alluding to the custom of holding more
than one living (pluralism, or being minister in more than one church).

206–207. *put you down*] (1) show himself cleverer than you by his
"wondrous wit"; (2) i.e., in bed.

209. *bankers*] persons engaged in tending the banks of a flooding river.

212. *needle's point*] of a compass.

LOLLIO.

> I could follow now as t'other fool did:
> "What should I fear,
> Having all joys about me? Do you but smile
> And love shall play the wanton on your lip,
> Meet and retire, retire and meet again;   225
> Look you but cheerfully, and in your eyes
> I shall behold my own deformity
> And dress myself up fairer. I know this shape
> Becomes me not—"
> And so as it follows. But is not this the more foolish way? 230
> Come, sweet rogue, kiss me, my little Lacedaemonian; let
> me feel how thy pulses beat. Thou hast a thing about thee
> would do a man pleasure, I'll lay my hand on't.

ISABELLA.

> Sirrah, no more; I see you have discovered
> This love's knight errant, who hath made adventure   235
> For purchase of my love; be silent, mute,
> Mute as a statue, or his injunction
> For me enjoying shall be to cut thy throat.
> I'll do it, though for no other purpose,
> And be sure he'll not refuse it.   240

LOLLIO.

> My share, that's all; I'll have my fool's part with you.

ISABELLA.

> No more, your master.

Enter Alibius.

ALIBIUS.   Sweet, how dost thou?

ISABELLA.

> Your bounden servant, sir.

ALIBIUS.   Fie, fie, sweetheart,
> No more of that.

ISABELLA.   You were best lock me up.

ALIBIUS.

> In my arms and bosom, my sweet Isabella,   245
> I'll lock thee up most nearly. Lollio,

---

233. *lay*] (1) wager; (2) place.
236. *purchase*] winning.

We have employment, we have task in hand;
At noble Vermandero's, our castle-captain,
There is a nuptial to be solemniz'd,
Beatrice Joanna his fair daughter, bride,   250
For which the gentleman hath bespoke our pains:
A mixture of our madmen and our fools
To finish, as it were, and make the fag
Of all the revels the third night from the first.
Only an unexpected passage over   255
To make a frightful pleasure, that is all,
But not the all I aim at. Could we so act it,
To teach it in a wild, distracted measure
Though out of form and figure, breaking time's head,
It were no matter; 'twould be heal'd again   260
In one age or other, if not in this;
This, this, Lollio, there's a good reward begun
And will beget a bounty, be it known.

LOLLIO.
This is easy, sir, I'll warrant you. You have about you fools
and madmen that can dance very well, and 'tis no wonder 265
your best dancers are not the wisest men; the reason is, with
often jumping they jolt their brains down into their feet, that
their wits lie more in their heels than in their heads.

ALIBIUS.
Honest Lollio, thou giv'st me a good reason
And a comfort in it.

ISABELLA.   Y'ave a fine trade on't: 270
Madmen and fools are a staple commodity.

ALIBIUS.
Oh, wife, we must eat, wear clothes, and live;
Just at the lawyers' haven we arrive,
By madmen and by fools we both do thrive.   *Exeunt.*

[III.iv]
        Enter Vermandero, Alsemero, Jasperino, *and* Beatrice.

VERMANDERO.
Valencia speaks so nobly of you, sir,

---

250. *bride*] i.e., being the bride.
253. *fag*] fag-end.
274. *thrive*] make our living.

I wish I had a daughter now for you.

ALSEMERO.

The fellow of this creature were a partner

For a king's love.

VERMANDERO.   I had her fellow once, sir,

But heaven has married her to joys eternal;   5

'Twere sin to wish her in this vale again.

Come, sir, your friend and you shall see the pleasures

Which my health chiefly joys in.

ALSEMERO.

I hear the beauty of this seat largely.

VERMANDERO.

It falls much short of that.   *Exeunt. Manet* Beatrice.

BEATRICE.   So, here's one step   10

Into my father's favor; time will fix him.

I have got him now the liberty of the house;

So wisdom by degrees works out her freedom.

And if that eye be darken'd that offends me

(I wait but that eclipse), this gentleman   15

Shall soon shine glorious in my father's liking

Through the refulgent virtue of my love.

Enter De Flores.

DE FLORES [*aside*].

My thoughts are at a banquet for the deed;

I feel no weight in't, 'tis but light and cheap

For the sweet recompense that I set down for't.   20

BEATRICE.

De Flores.

DE FLORES.   Lady.

BEATRICE.   Thy looks promise cheerfully.

DE FLORES.

All things are answerable: time, circumstance,

Your wishes, and my service.

BEATRICE.   Is it done then?

DE FLORES.

Piracquo is no more.

---

6. *vale*] i.e., of tears.

9. *largely*] at large; i.e., everywhere I go.

BEATRICE.
My joys start at mine eyes; our sweet'st delights   25
Are evermore born weeping.
DE FLORES.   I've a token for you.
BEATRICE.
For me?
DE FLORES.
But it was sent somewhat unwillingly;
I could not get the ring without the finger.
BEATRICE.
Bless me! What hast thou done?
DE FLORES.   Why, is that more   30
Than killing the whole man? I cut his heartstrings.
A greedy hand thrust in a dish at court
In a mistake hath had as much as this.
BEATRICE.
'Tis the first token my father made me send him.
DE FLORES.
And I made him send it back again   35
For his last token; I was loath to leave it,
And I'm sure dead men have no use of jewels.
He was as loath to part with't, for it stuck
As if the flesh and it were both one substance.
BEATRICE.
At the stag's fall the keeper has his fees;   40
'Tis soon applied: all dead men's fees are yours, sir.
I pray bury the finger, but the stone
You may make use on shortly; the true value,
Take't of my truth, is near three hundred ducats.
DE FLORES.
'Twill hardly buy a capcase for one's conscience though   45
To keep it from the worm, as fine as 'tis.
Well, being my fees I'll take it;
Great men have taught me that, or else my merit
Would scorn the way on't.

32–33. *A greedy . . . this*] If a person is greedy, he can lose a finger (from someone's knife) when he reaches into the dish for his food.

40. *At . . . fees*] The keeper (warden of a park, etc.) is traditionally given from the dead deer the skin, the head, and other parts (cf. 3 *Henry VI*, III.i.22).

45. *capcase*] small container.

BEATRICE.   It might justly, sir.
Why, thou mistak'st, De Flores; 'tis not given   50
In state of recompense.
DE FLORES.   No, I hope so, lady;
You should soon witness my contempt to't then.
BEATRICE.
Prithee, thou look'st as if thou wert offended.
DE FLORES.
That were strange, lady; 'tis not possible
My service should draw such a cause from you.   55
Offended? Could you think so? That were much
For one of my performance and so warm
Yet in my service.
BEATRICE.
'Twere misery in me to give you cause, sir.
DE FLORES.
I know so much; it were so, misery   60
In her most sharp condition.
BEATRICE.   'Tis resolv'd then.
Look you, sir, here's three thousand golden florins;
I have not meanly thought upon thy merit.
DE FLORES.
What, salary? Now you move me.
BEATRICE.   How, De Flores?
DE FLORES.
Do you place me in the rank of verminous fellows   65
To destroy things for wages? Offer gold?
The lifeblood of man! Is anything
Valued too precious for my recompense?
BEATRICE.
I understand thee not.
DE FLORES.   I could ha' hir'd
A journeyman in murder at this rate   70
And mine own conscience might have slept at ease
And have had the work brought home.

71. slept at ease] *Dilke; om. Q.*

---

51. *state*] way.
69–72. *I could . . . home*] The metaphor is commercial: the giving out of
piecework for later delivery to the contractor.
70. *journeyman*] i.e., professional.

BEATRICE [*aside*].   I'm in a labyrinth.
   What will content him? I would fain be rid of him.—
   I'll double the sum, sir.
DE FLORES.   You take a course
   To double my vexation, that's the good you do.   75
BEATRICE [*aside*].
   Bless me! I am now in worse plight than I was;
   I know not what will please him. —For my fear's sake
   I prithee make away with all speed possible;
   And if thou be'st so modest not to name
   The sum that will content thee, paper blushes not;   80
   Send thy demand in writing, it shall follow thee;
   But prithee take thy flight.
DE FLORES.   You must fly too, then.
BEATRICE.
   I?
DE FLORES.   I'll not stir a foot else.
BEATRICE.   What's your meaning?
DE FLORES.
   Why, are not you as guilty? In, I'm sure,
   As deep as I? And we should stick together.   85
   Come, your fears counsel you but ill; my absence
   Would draw suspect upon you instantly;
   There were no rescue for you.
BEATRICE [*aside*].   He speaks home.
DE FLORES.
   Nor is it fit we two engag'd so jointly
   Should part and live asunder.   [*Tries to kiss her.*]
BEATRICE.   How now, sir?   90
   This shows not well.
DE FLORES.   What makes your lip so strange?
   This must not be 'twixt us.
BEATRICE [*aside*].   The man talks wildly.
DE FLORES.
   Come, kiss me with a zeal, now.
BEATRICE [*aside*].   Heaven, I doubt him.

92. be 'twixt] *Neilson*; be betwixt
Q.

---

87. *suspect*] suspicion.

DE FLORES.
 I will not stand so long to beg 'em shortly.
BEATRICE.
 Take heed, De Flores, of forgetfulness;   95
 'Twill soon betray us.
DE FLORES.   Take you heed first;
 Faith, y'are grown much forgetful; y'are too blame in't.
BEATRICE [*aside*].
 He's bold, and I am blam'd for't.
DE FLORES.   I have eas'd
 You of your trouble, think on't; I'm in pain
 And must be eas'd of you; 'tis a charity.   100
 Justice invites your blood to understand me.
BEATRICE.
 I dare not.
DE FLORES. Quickly.
BEATRICE.   Oh, I never shall;
 Speak it yet further off, that I may lose
 What has been spoken and no sound remain on't.
 I would not hear so much offense again   105
 For such another deed.
DE FLORES.   Soft, lady, soft;
 The last is not yet paid for. Oh, this act
 Has put me into spirit; I was as greedy on't
 As the parch'd earth of moisture when the clouds weep.
 Did you not mark I wrought myself into't?   110
 Nay, sued and kneel'd for't? Why was all that pains took?
 You see I have thrown contempt upon your gold;
 Not that I want it not, for I do piteously;
 In order I will come unto't ànd make use on't.
 But 'twas not held so precious to begin with,   115
 For I place wealth after the heels of pleasure;
 And were I not resolv'd in my belief
 That thy virginity were perfect in thee,
 I should but take my recompense with grudging,
 As if I had but half my hopes I agreed for.   120

113. it not] *Dilke*; it *Q*.

---

97. *too blame*] too blameworthy; cf. II.ii.41.
99. *in pain*] suffering the pangs of love, as below, ll. 151–153.

BEATRICE.
  Why, 'tis impossible thou canst be so wicked
  Or shelter such a cunning cruelty,
  To make his death the murderer of my honor.
  Thy language is so bold and vicious
  I cannot see which way I can forgive it   125
  With any modesty.
DE FLORES.   Push, you forget yourself;
  A woman dipp'd in blood and talk of modesty!
BEATRICE.
  Oh, misery of sin! Would I had been bound
  Perpetually unto my living hate
  In that Piracquo than to hear these words.   130
  Think but upon the distance that creation
  Set 'twixt thy blood and mine, and keep thee there.
DE FLORES.
  Look but into your conscience, read me there;
  'Tis a true book; you'll find me there your equal.
  Push, fly not to your birth, but settle you   135
  In what the act has made you; y'are no more now.
  You must forget your parentage to me;
  Y'are the deed's creature; by that name
  You lost your first condition, and I challenge you,
  As peace and innocency has turn'd you out   140
  And made you one with me.
BEATRICE.   With thee, foul villain?
DE FLORES.
  Yes, my fair murderess; do you urge me?
  Though thou writ'st maid, thou whore in thy affection,
  'Twas chang'd from thy first love, and that's a kind
  Of whoredom in thy heart; and he's chang'd now   145
  To bring thy second on, thy Alsemero,
  Whom (by all sweets that ever darkness tasted),
  If I enjoy thee not, thou ne'er enjoy'st.

131–132. *the distance . . . mine*] the difference between our births now
demonstrated in the difference between our social positions.
  136. *no more*] i.e., than what the act has made you.
  137–138. *You . . . creature*] i.e., you are no longer the offspring of your
parents, you are now the offspring of the deed.
  145. *he's chang'd*] Alonzo's dead.

I'll blast the hopes and joys of marriage,
I'll confess all, my life I rate at nothing.   150
BEATRICE.
    De Flores.
DE FLORES.   I shall rest from all lovers' plagues then;
    I live in pain now. That shooting eye
    Will burn my heart to cinders.
BEATRICE.   Oh, sir, hear me.
DE FLORES.
    She that in life and love refuses me,
    In death and shame my partner she shall be.   155
BEATRICE.
    Stay, hear me once for all; I make thee master   [*Kneels.*]
    Of all the wealth I have in gold and jewels;
    Let me go poor unto my bed with honor
    And I am rich in all things.
DE FLORES.   Let this silence thee:
    The wealth of all Valencia shall not buy   160
    My pleasure from me.
    Can you weep fate from its determin'd purpose?
    So soon may you weep me.
BEATRICE.   Vengeance begins;
    Murder, I see, is followed by more sins.
    Was my creation in the womb so curs'd   165
    It must engender with a viper first?
DE FLORES.
    Come, rise and shroud your blushes in my bosom;   [*Raises her.*]
    Silence is one of pleasure's best receipts.
    Thy peace is wrought forever in this yielding.
    'Las, how the turtle pants! Thou'lt love anon   170
    What thou so fear'st and faint'st to venture on.   *Exeunt.*

Enter Gentlemen, Vermandero *meeting them with action of wonderment at
the flight of* Piracquo. *Enter* Alsemero *with* Jasperino *and Gallants;*
Vermandero *points to him, the Gentlemen seeming to applaud the choice.*

163. you] *Dyce; om. Q.*   171.1–9] *Q places this S.D. after the
                                    act designation of IV.*

165–166. *Was . . . first*] "Was a curse laid upon me [in the womb] that I
must engender [first] with . . . a viper?" (Bawcutt).
    168. *receipts*] recipes.   170. *turtle*] turtledove.

[*Exeunt in procession* Vermandero,] Alsemero, Jasperino, *and Gentle-*
men. [*Then enter*] Beatrice, *the Bride, following in great state, accompanied*
with Diaphanta, Isabella, *and other Gentlewomen.* [*Enter*] De Flores
after all, smiling at the accident. Alonzo's *Ghost appears to* De Flores *in the*
midst of his smile, startles him, showing him the hand whose finger he had cut
off. They pass over in great solemnity.

[IV.i]   *Enter* Beatrice.

BEATRICE.
    This fellow has undone me endlessly;
    Never was bride so fearfully distress'd.
    The more I think upon th'ensuing night
    And whom I am to cope with in embraces—
    One that's ennobled both in blood and mind,   5
    So clear in understanding (that's my plague now),
    Before whose judgment will my fault appear
    Like malefactors' crimes before tribunals,
    There is no hiding on't—the more I dive
    Into my own distress. How a wise man   10
    Stands for a great calamity! There's no venturing
    Into his bed (what course soe'er I light upon)
    Without my shame, which may grow up to danger.
    He cannot but in justice strangle me
    As I lie by him, as a cheater use me.   15
    'Tis a precious craft to play with a false die
    Before a cunning gamester. Here's his closet,
    The key left in't, and he abroad i'th' park;
    Sure, 'twas forgot; I'll be so bold as look in't.
    Bless me! A right physician's closet 'tis,   20
    Set round with vials; every one her mark, too.
    Sure, he does practice physic for his own use,
    Which may be safely call'd your great man's wisdom.
    What manuscript lies here? "The Book of Experiment,
    Call'd Secrets in Nature." So 'tis, 'tis so: 25

5. that's] *Bawcutt*; both *Q*.   15. by] *Dilke;* by by *Q*.

---

11. *Stands for*] Represents integrity in the face of (?).
22. *physic*] medicine.
24–25. "*The Book . . . Nature*"] *De Arcanis Naturae* by Antonius Mizaldus
(1520–1578). The tests are not in this work, but comparable ones are in
Mizaldus' *Centuriae IX. Memorabilium.*

"How to know whether a woman be with child or no."
I hope I am not yet. If he should try, though—
Let me see, folio forty-five. Here 'tis,
The leaf tuck'd down upon't, the place suspicious.
"If you would know whether a woman be with child or not,   30
give her two spoonfuls of the white water in glass C—"
Where's that glass C? Oh, yonder I see't now—
"and if she be with child, she sleeps full twelve hours after;
if not, not."
None of that water comes into my belly;   35
I'll know you from a hundred. I could break you now
Or turn you into milk and so beguile
The master of the mystery, but I'll look to you.
Ha! That which is next is ten times worse:
"How to know whether a woman be a maid or not."   40
If that should be applied, what would become of me?
Belike he has a strong faith of my purity
That never yet made proof, but this he calls
"A merry sleight but true experiment,
The author, Antonius Mizaldus":   45
"Give the party you suspect the quantity of a spoonful of
the water in the glass M which upon her that is a maid
makes three several effects: 'twill make her incontinently
gape, then fall into a sudden sneezing, last into a violent
laughing; else dull, heavy, and lumpish."   50
Where had I been?
I fear it, yet 'tis seven hours to bedtime.

Enter Diaphanta.

DIAPHANTA.
Cuds, madam, are you here?
BEATRICE [*aside*].   Seeing that wench now,
A trick comes in my mind; 'tis a nice piece
Gold cannot purchase. —I come hither, wench,   55
To look my lord.
DIAPHANTA.   Would I had such a cause

---

48. *incontinently*] instantly.
51. *Where . . . been?*] i.e., if I had not found this.
53. *Cuds*] i.e., God save me (Spencer).
54. *a nice piece*] "a scrupulous girl indeed" (Sampson).

To look him too. Why, he's i'th' park, madam.
BEATRICE.
There let him be.
DIAPHANTA.   Ay, madam, let him compass
Whole parks and forests as great rangers do;
At roosting time a little lodge can hold 'em.   60
Earth-conquering Alexander, that thought the world
Too narrow for him, in the end had but his pit-hole.
BEATRICE.
I fear thou art not modest, Diaphanta.
DIAPHANTA.
Your thoughts are so unwilling to be known, madam;
'Tis ever the bride's fashion towards bedtime   65
To set light by her joys as if she ow'd 'em not.
BEATRICE.
Her joys? Her fears, thou would'st say.
DIAPHANTA.   Fear of what?
BEATRICE.
Art thou a maid and talk'st so to a maid?
You leave a blushing business behind,
Beshrew your heart for't.
DIAPHANTA.   Do you mean good sooth, madam? 70
BEATRICE.
Well, if I'd thought upon the fear at first,
Man should have been unknown.
DIAPHANTA.   Is't possible?
BEATRICE.
I will give a thousand ducats to that woman
Would try what my fear were and tell me true
Tomorrow when she gets from't; as she likes,   75
I might perhaps be drawn to't.
DIAPHANTA.   Are you in earnest?
BEATRICE.
Do you get the woman, then challenge me,
And see if I'll fly from't; but I must tell you
This by the way, she must be a true maid
Else there's no trial, my fears are not hers else.   80

62. *pit-hole*] grave.
66. *ow'd*] owned.
79. *true maid*] real virgin.

DIAPHANTA.

Nay, she that I would put into your hands, madam,
Shall be a maid.

BEATRICE.   You know I should be sham'd else,
Because she lies for me.

DIAPHANTA.   'Tis a strange humor;
But are you serious still? Would you resign
Your first night's pleasure and give money too?   85

BEATRICE.

As willingly as live.—[*Aside.*]   Alas, the gold
Is but a by-bet to wedge in the honor.

DIAPHANTA.

I do not know how the world goes abroad
For faith or honesty; there's both requir'd in this.
Madam, what say you to me, and stray no further?   90
I've a good mind, in troth, to earn your money.

BEATRICE.

Y'are too quick, I fear, to be a maid.

DIAPHANTA.

How? Not a maid? Nay then, you urge me, madam,
Your honorable self is not a truer
With all your fears upon you—

BEATRICE [*aside*].   Bad enough then.   95

DIAPHANTA.

Than I with all my lightsome joys about me.

BEATRICE.

I'm glad to hear't; then you dare put your honesty
Upon an easy trial?

DIAPHANTA.   Easy? Anything.

BEATRICE.

I'll come to you straight.   [*Goes to the closet.*]

DIAPHANTA [*aside*].   She will not search me, will she?

97. hear't; then] *this edn.,* hear't
then, Q.

---

83. *humor*] whim.

87. *by-bet . . . honor*] side issue to insure that the important proof of my
chastity is carried out (?).

92. *quick*] gamesome, wanton.

99–100. *search . . . jury*] a topical reference to the divorce trial of the
Countess of Essex in 1613 during which she was medically examined by a
female jury.

Like the forewoman of a female jury?   100
BEATRICE.

Glass M, ay, this is it. —Look, Diaphanta,
You take no worse than I do.   [*Drinks.*]
DIAPHANTA.   And in so doing
I will not question what 'tis, but take it.   [*Drinks.*]
BEATRICE [*aside*].

Now if the experiment be true, 'twill praise itself
And give me noble ease. Begins already. [Diaphanta *gapes.*] 105
There's the first symptom; and what haste it makes
To fall into the second, there by this time. [Diaphanta *sneezes.*]
Most admirable secret. On the contrary,
It stirs not me a whit, which most concerns it.
DIAPHANTA.

Ha, ha, ha.
BEATRICE [*aside*].   Just in all things and in order   110
As if 'twere circumscrib'd, one accident
Gives way unto another.
DIAPHANTA.   Ha, ha, ha.
BEATRICE.

How now, wench?
DIAPHANTA.   Ha, ha, ha, I am so, so light
At heart, ha, ha, ha, so pleasurable.
But one swig more, sweet madam.
BEATRICE.   Ay, tomorrow;   115
We shall have time to sit by't.
DIAPHANTA.   Now I'm sad again.
BEATRICE [*aside*].

It lays itself so gently, too. —Come, wench,
Most honest Diaphanta I dare call thee now.
DIAPHANTA.

Pray tell me, madam, what trick call you this?
BEATRICE.

I'll tell thee all hereafter; we must study   120
The carriage of this business.
DIAPHANTA.   I shall carry't well
Because I love the burden.

---

111. *accident*] characteristic.

BEATRICE. About midnight
You must not fail to steal forth gently
That I may use the place.
DIAPHANTA. Oh, fear not, madam;
I shall be cool by that time. The bride's place 125
And with a thousand ducats! I'm for a justice now,
I bring a portion with me, I scorn small fools. *Exeunt.*

[IV.ii] *Enter* Vermandero *and Servant.*

VERMANDERO.
I tell thee, knave, mine honor is in question,
A thing till now free from suspicion,
Nor ever was there cause. Who of my Gentlemen
Are absent?
Tell me and truly how many and who. 5
SERVANT.
Antonio, sir, and Franciscus.
VERMANDERO.
When did they leave the castle?
SERVANT.
Some ten days since, sir; the one intending to Briamata,
th'other for Valencia.
VERMANDERO.
The time accuses 'em. A charge of murder 10
Is brought within my castle gate, Piracquo's murder;
I dare not answer faithfully their absence.
A strict command of apprehension
Shall pursue 'em suddenly and either wipe
The stain off clear or openly discover it. 15
Provide me winged warrants for the purpose.
See, I am set on again. *Exit* Servant.

Enter Tomazo.

TOMAZO.
I claim a brother of you.
VERMANDERO. Y'are too hot,

---

127. *portion*] dowry, marriage portion.
[IV.ii]
8. *Briamata*] Vermandero's country house in Reynolds's account.
12. *answer*] answer for.

Seek him not here.
TOMAZO.   Yes, 'mongst your dearest bloods;
If my peace find no fairer satisfaction,   20
This is the place must yield account for him,
For here I left him, and the hasty tie
Of this snatch'd marriage gives strong testimony
Of his most certain ruin.
VERMANDERO.   Certain falsehood!
This is the place indeed; his breach of faith   25
Has too much marr'd both my abused love,
The honorable love I reserv'd for him,
And mock'd my daughter's joy; the prepar'd morning
Blush'd at his infidelity; he left
Contempt and scorn to throw upon those friends   30
Whose belief hurt 'em. Oh, 'twas most ignoble
To take his flight so unexpectedly
And throw such public wrongs on those that lov'd him.
TOMAZO.
Then this is all your answer?
VERMANDERO.   'Tis too fair
For one of his alliance, and I warn you   35
That this place no more see you.   *Exit.*
TOMAZO.   The best is
There is more ground to meet a man's revenge on.

                    Enter De Flores.

Honest De Flores.
DE FLORES.   That's my name indeed.
Saw you the bride? Good sweet sir, which way took she?
TOMAZO.
I have bless'd mine eyes from seeing such a false one.   40
DE FLORES [*aside*].
I'd fain get off; this man's not for my company;
I smell his brother's blood when I come near him.
TOMAZO.
Come hither, kind and true one, I remember
My brother lov'd thee well.

37.1.] *after* see you (*l.* 36) *in* Q.

_____

31. *belief*] confidence in him.

                    – 65 –

DE FLORES.   Oh, purely, dear sir.—

    [*Aside.*]   Methinks I am now again a-killing on him,   45
    He brings it so fresh to me.

TOMAZO.   Thou canst guess, sirrah,
    One honest friend has an instinct of jealousy
    At some foul guilty person.

DE FLORES.   'Las sir,
    I am so charitable, I think none
    Worse than myself. You did not see the bride, then?   50

TOMAZO.
    I prithee name her not. Is she not wicked?

DE FLORES.
    No, no; a pretty, easy, round-pack'd sinner
    As your most ladies are, else you might think
    I flatter'd her; but, sir, at no hand wicked
    Till th'are so old their chins and noses meet   55
    And they salute witches. I am call'd, I think sir.—
    [*Aside.*]   His company ev'n o'erlays my conscience.   *Exit.*

TOMAZO.
    That De Flores has a wondrous honest heart;
    He'll bring it out in time, I'm assur'd on't.
    Oh, here's the glorious master of the day's joy;   60
    'Twill not be long till he and I do reckon.

                    Enter Alsemero.
    Sir.

ALSEMERO.   You are most welcome.

TOMAZO.   You may call that word back;
    I do not think I am, nor wish to be.

ALSEMERO.
    'Tis strange you found the way to this house then.

TOMAZO.
    Would I'd ne'er known the cause. I'm none of those, sir,   65
    That come to give you joy and swill your wine;
    'Tis a more precious liquor that must lay

---

55. chins and noses] *Dyce*; sins and   61. 'Twill] *Dilke*; I will *Q*.
vices *Q*.   61.1.] *after* Sir (*l.* 62) *in Q*.

---

    52. *easy . . . sinner*] comfortably and plumply full of sin.
    54–56. *at . . . witches*] they are not really wicked until they are so old
they consort with witches.

The fiery thirst I bring.
ALSEMERO.   Your words and you
Appear to me great strangers.
TOMAZO.   Time and our swords
May make us more acquainted. This the business: 70
I should have a brother in your place;
How treachery and malice have dispos'd of him
I'm bound to inquire of him which holds his right,
Which never could come fairly.
ALSEMERO.   You must look
To answer for that word, sir.
TOMAZO.   Fear you not;   75
I'll have it ready drawn at our next meeting.
Keep your day solemn; farewell, I disturb it not.
I'll bear the smart with patience for a time.   *Exit.*
ALSEMERO.
'Tis somewhat ominous, this, a quarrel enter'd
Upon this day; my innocence relieves me,   80

Enter Jasperino.

I should be wondrous sad else. Jasperino,
I have news to tell thee, strange news.
JASPERINO.   I ha' some too,
I think as strange as yours; would I might keep
Mine, so my faith and friendship might be kept in't.
Faith, sir, dispense a little with my zeal   85
And let it cool in this.
ALSEMERO.   This puts me on
And blames thee for thy slowness.
JASPERINO.   All may prove nothing,
Only a friendly fear that leap'd from me, sir.
ALSEMERO.
No question it may prove nothing; let's partake it, though.

89. though] tho *Q* (*uncorr.*); thou
Q (*corr.*).

---

75. *that word*] i.e., the charge of unfairness or dishonesty.
76. *it*] my sword; as if it were an official answer, "drawn" up.
85–86. *dispense . . . this*] i.e., if you would allow the vigor of my friendship
and service to grow somewhat slack ("cool"), I should not have to pass on
this news.

JASPERINO.

'Twas Diaphanta's chance (for to that wench   90
I pretend honest love, and she deserves it)
To leave me in a back part of the house,
A place we chose for private conference;
She was no sooner gone, but instantly
I heard your bride's voice in the next room to me   95
And, lending more attention, found De Flores
Louder than she.

ALSEMERO.   De Flores? Thou art out now.

JASPERINO.

You'll tell me more anon.

ALSEMERO.   Still I'll prevent thee:
The very sight of him is poison to her.

JASPERINO.

That made me stagger too, but Diaphanta   100
At her return confirm'd it.

ALSEMERO.   Diaphanta!

JASPERINO.

Then fell we both to listen, and words pass'd
Like those that challenge interest in a woman.

ALSEMERO.

Peace, quench thy zeal; 'tis dangerous to thy bosom.

JASPERINO.

Then truth is full of peril.

ALSEMERO.   Such truths are;   105
Oh, were she the sole glory of the earth,
Had eyes that could shoot fire into kings' breasts,
And touch'd, she sleeps not here; yet I have time,
Though night be near, to be resolv'd hereof,
And prithee do not weigh me by my passions.   110

JASPERINO.

I never weigh'd friend so.

ALSEMERO.   Done charitably.

91. *pretend*] proffer.
97. *out*] mistaken; i.e., out of the area of the believable, or out of your part.
98. *Still . . . thee*] I'll explain it again and more explicitly so as to forestall your improbable news.
108. *touch'd*] tainted.

That key will lead thee to a pretty secret   [*Gives key.*]
By a Chaldean taught me, and I've made
My study upon some. Bring from my closet
A glass inscrib'd there with the letter M,   115
And question not my purpose.
JASPERINO.   It shall be done, sir.   *Exit.*
ALSEMERO.
How can this hang together? Not an hour since
Her woman came pleading her lady's fears,
Deliver'd her for the most timorous virgin
That ever shrunk at man's name and so modest   120
She charg'd her weep out her request to me
That she might come obscurely to my bosom.

Enter Beatrice.

BEATRICE [*aside*].
All things go well. My woman's preparing yonder
For her sweet voyage which grieves me to lose;
Necessity compels it, I lose all else.   125
ALSEMERO [*aside*].
Push, modesty's shrine is set in yonder forehead;
I cannot be too sure, though. —My Joanna.
BEATRICE.
Sir, I was bold to weep a message to you;
Pardon my modest fears.
ALSEMERO [*aside*].   The dove's not meeker;
She's abus'd questionless.—

Enter Jasperino.

                        Oh, are you come, sir? 130
BEATRICE [*aside*].
The glass, upon my life; I see the letter.
JASPERINO.
Sir, this is M.
ALSEMERO.   'Tis it.
BEATRICE [*aside*].   I am suspected.

113. made] *Bawcutt*; *om. Q.*   130. S.D.] *after* sir (*l.* 130) *in* Q.

113. *a Chaldean*] one of an ancient tribe of seers and wizards.
122. *obscurely*] in the dark.

ALSEMERO.
>How fitly our bride comes to partake with us.

BEATRICE.
>What is't, my lord?

ALSEMERO.   No hurt.

BEATRICE.   Sir, pardon me,
>I seldom taste of any composition.   135

ALSEMERO.
>But this upon my warrant you shall venture on.

BEATRICE.
>I fear 'twill make me ill.

ALSEMERO.   Heaven forbid that.

BEATRICE [aside].
>I'm put now to my cunning; th'effects I know,
>If I can now but feign 'em handsomely.

ALSEMERO [aside].
>It has that secret virtue it ne'er miss'd, sir,   140
>Upon a virgin.

JASPERINO [aside].   Treble qualitied.

>   [Beatrice gapes, then sneezes.]

ALSEMERO [aside].
>By all that's virtuous! It takes there, proceeds.

JASPERINO [aside].
>This is the strangest trick to know a maid by.

BEATRICE.
>Ha, ha, ha,
>You have given me joy of heart to drink, my lord.   145

ALSEMERO.
>No, thou hast given me such joy of heart
>That never can be blasted.

BEATRICE.   What's the matter, sir?

ALSEMERO [aside].
>See now, 'tis settl'd in a melancholy
>Keeps both the time and method. —My Joanna,
>Chaste as the breath of heaven or morning's womb   150
>That brings the day forth, thus my love encloses thee.

>   [He embraces her.] Exeunt.

149. Keeps] *Dyce*; Keep *Q*.

---

135. *composition*] mixture.

[IV.iii]   *Enter* Isabella *and* Lollio.

ISABELLA.

Oh heaven! Is this the waxing moon?
Does love turn fool, run mad, and all at once?
Sirrah, here's a madman akin to the fool, too,
A lunatic lover.

LOLLIO.

No, no, not he I brought the letter from?   5

ISABELLA.

Compare his inside with his out and tell me.

LOLLIO.

The out's mad, I'm sure of that, I had a taste on't.   [*Reads
letter.*] "To the bright Andromeda, chief chambermaid to
the knight of the sun, at the sign of Scorpio in the middle
region, sent by the bellows-mender of Aeolus. Pay the post."   10
This is stark madness.

ISABELLA.

Now mark the inside.   [*Takes letter and reads.*] "Sweet lady,
having now cast off this counterfeit cover of a madman,
I appear to your best judgment a true and faithful lover
of your beauty."   15

LOLLIO.

He is mad still.

ISABELLA [*reads*].

"If any fault you find, chide those perfections in you which

1. waxing] *this edn.;* waiting *Q.*   2. at] *Dilke; om. Q.*
See Appendix A.

---

1. *waxing*] i.e., causing thereby an increase of lunacy.
7. *taste*] presumably Franciscus' show of violence against Lollio (III.iii.
84 S.D.).
8–10. *Andromeda . . . Aeolus*] "Isabella is addressed as Andromeda presumably because Franciscus is the Perseus who is to rescue her from the
dragon Alibius. In his character of "A Chamber-Mayde" (whom he describes as being extremely lascivious), Overbury says of her that 'Shee . . .
is so carried away with the *Myrrour of Knighthood* [a popular chivalric rom-
ance], [that] she is many times resolv'd to . . . become a Ladie Errant.' . . .
The Knight of the Sun is one of the heroes of the work. . . . Scorpio was the
sign [of the zodiac] governing the privy parts of the body, and this turns
'middle region', an astronomical term, into an obvious pun" (Bawcutt).
Aeolus is the god of the winds.

have made me imperfect; 'tis the same sun that causeth to
grow and enforceth to wither—"

LOLLIO.

Oh, rogue!   20

ISABELLA [*reads*].

"Shapes and transshapes, destroys and builds again. I come
in winter to you dismantled of my proper ornaments; by the
sweet splendor of your cheerful smiles, I spring and live a
lover."

LOLLIO.

Mad rascal still.   25

ISABELLA [*reads*].

"Tread him not underfoot, that shall appear an honor to
your bounties. I remain, mad till I speak with you from
whom I expect my cure, yours all, or one beside himself,
Franciscus."

LOLLIO.

You are like to have a fine time on't; my master and I may   30
give over our professions; I do not think but you can cure
fools and madmen faster than we, with little pains too.

ISABELLA.

Very likely.

LOLLIO.

One thing I must tell you, mistress: you perceive that I am
privy to your skill; if I find you minister once and set up the   35
trade, I put in for my thirds, I shall be mad or fool else.

ISABELLA.

The first place is thine, believe it, Lollio,
If I do fall—

LOLLIO.

I fall upon you.

ISABELLA.

So.   40

LOLLIO.

Well, I stand to my venture.

ISABELLA.

But thy counsel now; how shall I deal with 'em?

18. have] *Dilke*; *have have Q*.

35–36. *minister . . . trade*] become a prostitute, commit adultery.
42, 43. *deal with*] (1) treat, handle; (2) have illicit relations with.

LOLLIO.

Why, do you mean to deal with 'em?

ISABELLA.

Nay, the fair understanding; how to use 'em.

LOLLIO.

Abuse 'em; that's the way to mad the fool and make a fool of   45
the madman, and then you use 'em kindly.

ISABELLA.

'Tis easy, I'll practice; do thou observe it.
The key of thy wardrobe.

LOLLIO.

There; fit yourself for 'em, and I'll fit 'em both for you.

ISABELLA.

Take thou no further notice than the outside.   *Exit.*   50

LOLLIO.

Not an inch; I'll put you to the inside.

Enter Alibius.

ALIBIUS.

Lollio, art there? Will all be perfect, think'st thou?
Tomorrow night as if to close up the solemnity
Vermandero expects us.

LOLLIO.

I mistrust the madmen most; the fools will do well enough,   55
I have taken pains with them.

ALIBIUS.

Tush, they cannot miss; the more absurdity,
The more commends it; so no rough behaviors
Affright the ladies; they are nice things, thou know'st.

LOLLIO.

You need not fear, sir; so long as we are there with our com-   60
manding pizzles, they'll be as tame as the ladies themselves.

ALIBIUS.

I will see them once more rehearse before they go.

43. Why, do] *Dilke*; We do *Q*.

---

44. *the fair understanding*] "understand my speeches in the fair and modest
sense in which they are uttered" (Dilke).

46. *kindly*] (1) gently; (2) naturally.

53. *solemnity*] ceremony.

61. *pizzles*] dried penises (generally of bulls) used as whips.

LOLLIO.

I was about it, sir; look you to the madmen's morris, and
let me alone with the other. There is one or two that I
mistrust their fooling; I'll instruct them, and then they shall   65
rehearse the whole measure.

ALIBIUS.

Do so; I'll see the music prepar'd. But, Lollio,
By the way, how does my wife brook her restraint?
Does she not grudge at it?

LOLLIO.

So, so; she takes some pleasure in the house; she would   70
abroad else. You must allow her a little more length;
she's kept too short.

ALIBIUS.

She shall along to Vermandero's with us;
That will serve her for a month's liberty.

LOLLIO.

What's that on your face, sir?   75

ALIBIUS.

Where, Lollio? I see nothing.

LOLLIO.

Cry you mercy, sir, 'tis your nose; it show'd like the trunk
of a young elephant.

ALIBIUS.

Away, rascal; I'll prepare the music, Lollio.   *Exit* Alibius.

LOLLIO.

Do, sir, and I'll dance the whilst. —Tony, where art   80
thou, Tony?

Enter Antonio.

ANTONIO.

Here, cousin: where art thou?

LOLLIO.

Come, Tony, the footmanship I taught you.

ANTONIO.

I had rather ride, cousin.

---

63. *morris*] country dance.
77–78. *nose . . . elephant*] the long nose may signify that Alibius is being
led by the nose (?).

LOLLIO.

    Ay, a whip take you, but I'll keep you out. Vault in; look you,   85

    Tony, fa, la la la la.   [*Dances.*]

ANTONIO.

    Fa, la la la la.   [*Dances.*]

LOLLIO.

    There an honor.

ANTONIO.

    Is this an honor, coz?

LOLLIO.

    Yes, and it please your worship.   90

ANTONIO.

    Does honor bend in the hams, coz?

LOLLIO.

    Marry does it, as low as worship, squireship, nay, yeomanry

    itself sometimes, from whence it first stiffened. There rise

    a caper.

ANTONIO.

    Caper after an honor, coz?   95

LOLLIO.

    Very proper, for honor is but a caper, rises as fast and high,

    has a knee or two, and falls to th' ground again. You can

    remember your figure, Tony?   *Exit.*

ANTONIO.

    Yes, cousin; when I see thy figure, I can remember mine.

                                           [*Dances.*]

       Enter Isabella [*dressed as a madwoman*].

ISABELLA.

    Hey, how he treads the air; shoo, shoo, t'other way, he 100

96. rises] *Dilke*; rise *Q*.   100. how he] *Dilke*; how she *Q*.

---

   88. *honor*] bow, obeisance.

   94. *caper*] an upward leap.

   98, 99. *figure*] (1) dance pattern; (2) face.

   100–121. *Hey . . . my love*] Seeing Antonio dancing, Isabella imagines that he is Icarus flying from imprisonment in Crete on wings made by his father, Daedalus. Icarus flew too high, the sun melted the wax holding the feathers to the wings, and he fell into the sea where he drowned.

   100. *treads the air*] i.e., dances or flies.

   100. *shoo*] an exclamation to drive away poultry.

burns his wings else; here's wax enough below, Icarus, more
than will be canceled these eighteen moons.   [Antonio *falls*.]
He's down, he's down; what a terrible fall he had.
Stand up, thou son of Cretan Daedalus,
And let us tread the lower labyrinth;   105
I'll bring thee to the clue.   [Antonio *rises*.]

ANTONIO.

Prithee, coz, let me alone.

ISABELLA.

Art thou not drown'd?
About thy head I saw a heap of clouds,
Wrapp'd like a Turkish turban; on thy back   110
A crook'd, chameleon-color'd rainbow hung
Like a tiara down unto thy hams.
Let me suck out those billows in thy belly;
Hark how they roar and rumble in the straits.
Bless thee from the pirates.   115

ANTONIO.

Pox upon you; let me alone.

ISABELLA.

Why should'st thou mount so high as Mercury
Unless thou hadst reversion of his place?
Stay in the moon with me, Endymion,
And we will rule these wild rebellious waves   120

114. straits] *Dyce*; streets *Q*.

101–102. *wax . . . canceled*] the wax on Icarus' wings reminds Isabella
(irrelevantly) of the seals on legal documents (perhaps her marriage
contract?).

105. *lower labyrinth*] i.e., the maze on earth, not the ways of the air.

105–106. *labyrinth . . . clue*] According to one version of the myth,
Daedalus and Icarus were imprisoned in the labyrinth from which they
escaped by flight; according to another, the labyrinth confined a monster
slain by Theseus, to whom Ariadne had given a thread ("clue") by which he
could find his way back out.

113, 114, 115, 120. *billows, straits, pirates, waves*] References to the Icarian
Sea in which Icarus drowned.

117. *Mercury*] the messenger and herald of the gods.

118. *thou . . . place*] you were to be his successor.

119. *Endymion*] a shepherd youth beloved by Luna; here Isabella sees
herself as the moon-goddess, controlling the tides.

That would have drown'd my love.

ANTONIO.

I'll kick thee if again thou touch me,
Thou wild unshapen antic; I am no fool,
You bedlam.

ISABELLA.   But you are as sure as I am, mad.

Have I put on this habit of a frantic   125
With love as full of fury to beguile
The nimble eye of watchful jealousy,
And am I thus rewarded?

ANTONIO.

Ha, dearest beauty.

ISABELLA.   No, I have no beauty now,

Nor never had, but what was in my garments.   130
You a quick-sighted lover? Come not near me.
Keep your caparisons, y'are aptly clad;
I came a feigner to return stark mad.   *Exit.*

Enter Lollio.

ANTONIO.

Stay, or I shall change condition
And become as you are.   135

LOLLIO.

Why, Tony, whither now? Why, fool—

ANTONIO.

Whose fool, usher of idiots? You coxcomb,
I have fool'd too much.

LOLLIO.

You were best be mad another while then.

ANTONIO.

So I am, stark mad, I have cause enough;   140
And I could throw the full effects on thee
And beat thee like a fury.

LOLLIO.

Do not, do not; I shall not forbear the gentleman under the

123. *antic*] clown.
132. *caparisons*] clothes.
137. *usher*] (1) doorkeeper; (2) subordinate teacher.

fool, if you do. Alas, I saw through your fox-skin before now.
Come, I can give you comfort: my mistress loves you, and 145
there is as arrant a madman i'th' house as you are a fool,
your rival, whom she loves not. If after the masque we can
rid her of him, you earn her love, she says, and the fool shall
ride her.

ANTONIO.

May I believe thee?   150

LOLLIO.

Yes, or you may choose whether you will or no.

ANTONIO.

She's eas'd of him; I have a good quarrel on't.

LOLLIO.

Well, keep your old station yet, and be quiet.

ANTONIO.

Tell her I will deserve her love.

LOLLIO.

And you are like to have your desire.   [*Exit* Antonio.] 155

Enter Franciscus.

FRANCISCUS [*sings*].

Down, down, down a-down a-down, and then with a horse-trick
To kick Latona's forehead and break her bowstring.

LOLLIO.

This is t'other counterfeit; I'll put him out of his humor.
[*Reads.*] "Sweet lady, having now cast off this counterfeit
cover of a madman, I appear to your best judgment a true 160
and faithful lover of your beauty."—This is pretty well for
a madman.

FRANCISCUS.

Ha! What's that?

LOLLIO [*reads*].

"Chide those perfections in you which have made me imperfect."

159. off] *Dyce*; *om. Q*.   164. have] *Dyce*; *om. Q*.

---

144. *fox-skin*] clothes concealing fox-like cunning.

157. *Latona's* . . . *bowstring*] Latona is here taken as another name for the
moon-goddess who (represented by Diana, the huntress) carried a bow;
actually, Latona was Diana's mother.

FRANCISCUS.
I am discover'd to the fool.   165
LOLLIO.
I hope to discover the fool in you ere I have done with
you. —[*Reads.*] "Yours all, or one beside himself,
Franciscus."—This madman will mend sure.
FRANCISCUS.
What do you read, sirrah?
LOLLIO.
Your destiny, sir; you'll be hang'd for this trick and another 170
that I know.
FRANCISCUS.
Art thou of counsel with thy mistress?
LOLLIO.
Next her apron strings.
FRANCISCUS.
Give me thy hand.
LOLLIO.
Stay, let me put yours in my pocket first. [*Puts up letter.*] 175
Your hand is true, is it not? It will not pick? I partly fear it,
because I think it does lie.
FRANCISCUS.
Not in a syllable.
LOLLIO.
So, if you love my mistress so well as you have handled the
matter here, you are like to be cur'd of your madness.   180
FRANCISCUS.
And none but she can cure it.
LOLLIO.
Well, I'll give you over then, and she shall cast your water
next.
FRANCISCUS.
Take for thy pains past.   [*Gives money.*]
LOLLIO.
I shall deserve more, sir, I hope. My mistress loves you,   185
but must have some proof of your love to her.

---

175. *yours*] your handwriting; the letter.
176. *pick*] steal.
182. *cast . . . water*] analyze urine as a part of medical diagnosis.

FRANCISCUS.

There I meet my wishes.

LOLLIO.

That will not serve; you must meet her enemy and yours.

FRANCISCUS.

He's dead already.

LOLLIO.

Will you tell me that, and I parted but now with him?   190

FRANCISCUS.

Show me the man.

LOLLIO.

Ay, that's a right course now, see him before you kill him in
any case; and yet it needs not go so far neither, 'tis but a fool
that haunts the house and my mistress in the shape of an
idiot. Bang but his fool's coat well-favoredly, and 'tis well. 195

FRANCISCUS.

Soundly, soundly.

LOLLIO.

Only reserve him till the masque be past, and if you find
him not now in the dance yourself, I'll show you. In, in;
my master.

FRANCISCUS.

He handles him like a feather. Hey!   [*Exit dancing.*] 200

Enter Alibius.

ALIBIUS.

Well said; in a readiness, Lollio?

LOLLIO.

Yes, sir.

ALIBIUS.

Away then, and guide them in, Lollio;
Entreat your mistress to see this sight.
Hark, is there not one incurable fool   205
That might be begg'd? I have friends.

LOLLIO.

I have him for you, one that shall deserve it too.

---

201. *Well said*] well done.
205–206. *fool . . . begg'd*] "To beg a fool was to seek appointment as
his guardian and thus enjoy his estate" (Schelling).

ALIBIUS.

Good boy, Lollio.   [*Exit* Lollio.]

[*Enter* Isabella; *then enter* Lollio *with Madmen and Fools.*] *The Madmen and Fools dance.*

'Tis perfect; well, fit but once these strains,
We shall have coin and credit for our pains.   *Exeunt.* 210

[V.i]   *Enter* Beatrice. *A clock strikes one.*

BEATRICE.

One struck, and yet she lies by't. Oh, my fears,
This strumpet serves her own ends, 'tis apparent now,
Devours the pleasure with a greedy appetite
And never minds my honor or my peace,
Makes havoc of my right; but she pays dearly for't,   5
No trusting of her life with such a secret,
That cannot rule her blood to keep her promise.
Beside, I have some suspicion of her faith to me
Because I was suspected of my lord,
And it must come from her. Hark, by my horrors,   10
Another clock strikes two.   *Strikes two.*

Enter De Flores.

DE FLORES.   Pist, where are you?
BEATRICE.

De Flores?
DE FLORES.   Ay; is she not come from him yet?
BEATRICE.

As I am a living soul not.
DE FLORES.   Sure the devil
Hath sow'd his itch within her; who'd trust
A waiting-woman?
BEATRICE.   I must trust somebody.   15
DE FLORES.

Push, they are termagants.
Especially when they fall upon their masters

[V.i]
11. S.D. *Strikes*] *Dilke*; *Strike* Q.

_____

209. *these strains*] this music.

−81−

And have their ladies' first-fruits, th'are mad whelps;
You cannot stave 'em off from game royal then.
You are so harsh and hardy, ask no counsel;   20
And I could have help'd you to an apothecary's daughter
Would have fall'n off before eleven and thank'd you too.

BEATRICE.

Oh me, not yet? This whore forgets herself.

DE FLORES.

The rascal fares so well; look, y'are undone,
The day-star, by this hand. See Phosphorus plain yonder.   25

BEATRICE.

Advise me now to fall upon some ruin;
There is no counsel safe else.

DE FLORES.   Peace; I ha't now;
For we must force a rising; there's no remedy.

BEATRICE.

How? Take heed of that.

DE FLORES.   Tush, be you quiet
Or else give over all.

BEATRICE.   Prithee, I ha' done then.   30

DE FLORES.

This is my reach: I'll set some part afire
Of Diaphanta's chamber.

BEATRICE   How? Fire, sir?
That may endanger the whole house.

DE FLORES.

You talk of danger when your fame's on fire?

BEATRICE.

That's true; do what thou wilt now.

DE FLORES.   Push, I aim   35
At a most rich success, strikes all dead sure.
The chimney being afire and some light parcels

---

21. an] *Dilke*; a *Q*.   25. Phosphorus] *Dilke*; *Bosphorus*
22. thank'd] *Dilke*; thank *Q*.   *Q*.

---

25. *Phosphorus*] the morning star.
26. *fall . . . ruin*] come upon some method of destruction (of myself?).
28. *rising*] i.e., of the entire household.
31. *reach*] plan.
34. *fame*] reputation (the original Latin meaning).

Of the least danger in her chamber only,
If Diaphanta should be met by chance then
Far from her lodging, which is now suspicious,   40
It would be thought her fears and affrights then
Drove her to seek for succor; if not seen
Or met at all, as that's the likeliest,
For her own shame she'll hasten towards her lodging.
I will be ready with a piece high-charg'd   45
As 'twere to cleanse the chimney. There, 'tis proper now;
But she shall be the mark.
BEATRICE.   I'm forc'd to love thee now,
'Cause thou provid'st so carefully for my honor.
DE FLORES.
'Slid, it concerns the safety of us both,
Our pleasure and continuance.   50
BEATRICE.
One word now, prithee: how for the servants?
DE FLORES.
I'll dispatch them, some one way, some another,
In the hurry, for buckets, hooks, ladders;
Fear not you;
The deed shall find its time, and I've thought since   55
Upon a safe conveyance for the body too.
How this fire purifies wit! Watch you your minute.
BEATRICE.
Fear keeps my soul upon't; I cannot stray from't.

Enter Alonzo's Ghost.

DE FLORES.
Ha! What art thou that tak'st away the light
'Twixt that star and me? I dread thee not.   60
'Twas but a mist of conscience; all's clear again.   *Exit.*
BEATRICE.
Who's that, De Flores? Bless me! It slides by;   [*Exit Ghost.*]
Some ill thing haunts the house; 't has left behind it
A shivering sweat upon me. I'm afraid now.
This night hath been so tedious. Oh, this strumpet!   65

45. *piece*] gun.
49. *'Slid*] By God's eyelid.

Had she a thousand lives, he should not leave her
Till he had destroy'd the last. List, oh my terrors,
Three struck by St. Sebastian's.   *Strikes three.*
DE FLORES (*within*).   Fire, fire, fire.
BEATRICE.
    Already! How rare is that man's speed!
    How heartily he serves me! His face loathes one,   70
    But look upon his care, who would not love him?
    The east is not more beauteous than his service.
DE FLORES (*within*).
    Fire, fire, fire.

            Enter De Flores. *Servants pass over*; *ring a bell.*

DE FLORES.
    Away, dispatch; hooks, buckets, ladders; that's well said.
    The fire bell rings, the chimney works; my charge,   75
    The piece is ready.   *Exit.*
BEATRICE.   Here's a man worth loving.

            Enter Diaphanta.

    Oh, y'are a jewel.
DIAPHANTA.   Pardon frailty, madam;
    In troth I was so well, I e'en forgot myself.
BEATRICE.
    Y'have made trim work.
DIAPHANTA.   What?
BEATRICE.   Hie quickly to your chamber,
    Your reward follows you.
DIAPHANTA.   I never made   80
    So sweet a bargain.   *Exit.*

            Enter Alsemero.

68. S.D. *Strikes three.*] *this edn.*;   73. S.P. DE FLORES.] *this edn.*;
Struck 3 a clock. Q.   *Within Q.*
68. S.P. DE FLORES.] *this edn.*;   73.1. De Flores. *Servants*] *Dilke*;
Within Q.   *Deflores servants: Q.*
                                             76.1.] *after* ready (*l.* 76) *in Q.*

66. *he*] De Flores.
70. *loathes*] disgusts.
74, 89. *well said*] well done.

ALSEMERO.   Oh, my dear Joanna;
Alas, art thou risen too? I was coming,
My absolute treasure—
BEATRICE.   When I missed you,
I could not choose but follow.
ALSEMERO.   Th'art all sweetness.
The fire is not so dangerous.
BEATRICE.   Think you so, sir?   85
ALSEMERO.
I prithee, tremble not; believe me, 'tis not.

Enter Vermandero, Jasperino.

VERMANDERO.
Oh, bless my house and me.
ALSEMERO.   My lord your father.

Enter De Flores *with a piece.*

VERMANDERO.
Knave, whither goes that piece?
DE FLORES.   To scour the chimney.   *Exit.*
VERMANDERO.
Oh, well said, well said;
That fellow's good on all occasions.   90
BEATRICE.
A wondrous necessary man, my lord.
VERMANDERO.
He hath a ready wit; he's worth 'em all, sir.
Dog at a house of fire; I ha' seen him sing'd ere now.
                    The piece goes off.
Ha, there he goes.
BEATRICE.
'Tis done.   95
ALSEMERO.
Come sweet, to bed now; alas, thou wilt get cold.
BEATRICE.
Alas, the fear keeps that out;
My heart will find no quiet till I hear
How Diaphanta, my poor woman, fares;

---

93. *Dog at*] keen; i.e., like a dog in pursuit.

It is her chamber, sir, her lodging chamber.   100
VERMANDERO.
How should the fire come there?
BEATRICE.
As good a soul as ever lady countenanc'd,
But in her chamber negligent and heavy.
She 'scap'd a mine twice.
VERMANDERO.   Twice?
BEATRICE.   Strangely, twice, sir.
VERMANDERO.
Those sleepy sluts are dangerous in a house,   105
And they be ne'er so good.

Enter De Flores.

DE FLORES.   Oh, poor virginity!
Thou hast paid dearly for't.
VERMANDERO.   Bless us! What's that?
DE FLORES.
A thing you all knew once; Diaphanta's burnt.
BEATRICE.
My woman, oh, my woman!
DE FLORES.   Now the flames are
Greedy of her; burnt, burnt, burnt to death, sir.   110
BEATRICE.
Oh, my presaging soul!
ALSEMERO.   Not a tear more,
I charge you by the last embrace I gave you
In bed before this rais'd us.
BEATRICE.   Now you tie me;
Were it my sister now, she gets no more.

Enter Servant.

VERMANDERO.
How now?
SERVANT.   All danger's past; you may now take   115
Your rests, my lords; the fire is throughly quench'd.
Ah, poor gentlewoman, how soon was she stifled!

---

103. *heavy*] slovenly.
104. *mine*] particular danger (unspecified).

BEATRICE.

De Flores, what is left of her inter,
And we as mourners all will follow her.
I will entreat that honor to my servant   120
E'en of my lord himself.

ALSEMERO.   Command it, sweetness.

BEATRICE.

Which of you spied the fire first?

DE FLORES.   'Twas I, madam.

BEATRICE.

And took such pains in't too? A double goodness!
'Twere well he were rewarded.

VERMANDERO.   He shall be;
De Flores, call upon me.

ALSEMERO.   And upon me, sir.   125

Exeunt [all but De Flores].

DE FLORES.

Rewarded? Precious, here's a trick beyond me;
I see in all bouts both of sport and wit
Always a woman strives for the last hit.   *Exit.*

[V.ii]   *Enter* Tomazo.

TOMAZO.

I cannot taste the benefits of life
With the same relish I was wont to do.
Man I grow weary of and hold his fellowship
A treacherous bloody friendship, and because
I am ignorant in whom my wrath should settle,   5
I must think all men villains, and the next
I meet, whoe'er he be, the murderer
Of my most worthy brother. Ha! What's he?

Enter De Flores, *passes over the stage.*

Oh, the fellow that some call honest De Flores.
But methinks honesty was hard bested   10
To come there for a lodging; as if a queen
Should make her palace of a pest-house.
I find a contrariety in nature

[V.ii]
  10. *hard bested*] hard put to it.

Betwixt that face and me; the least occasion
Would give me game upon him; yet he's so foul   15
One would scarce touch him with a sword he loved
And made account of. So most deadly venemous,
He would go near to poison any weapon
That should draw blood on him; one must resolve
Never to use that sword again in fight   20
In way of honest manhood that strikes him;
Some river must devour't, 'twere not fit
That any man should find it. What, again?

Enter De Flores.

He walks o' purpose by, sure, to choke me up,
To infect my blood.

DE FLORES.   My worthy noble lord.   25

TOMAZO.

Dost offer to come near and breathe upon me?   [*Strikes him.*]

DE FLORES.

A blow.   [*Draws his sword.*]

TOMAZO.   Yea; are you so prepar'd?
I'll rather like a soldier die by th' sword
Than like a politician by thy poison.

DE FLORES.

Hold, my lord, as you are honorable.   30

TOMAZO.

All slaves that kill by poison are still cowards.

DE FLORES [*aside*].

I cannot strike, I see his brother's wounds
Fresh bleeding in his eye as in a crystal.—
I will not question this, I know y'are noble;
I take my injury with thanks given, sir,   35
Like a wise lawyer; and as a favor
Will wear it for the worthy hand that gave it.—
[*Aside.*]   Why this from him that yesterday appear'd
So strangely loving to me?
Oh, but instinct is of a subtler strain.   40

16. him] *Dilke*; *om. Q.*   18. near] *Dyce*; ne're *Q.*

---

15. *give me game*] "incite me to fight" (Sampson).
29. *politician*] intriguer, schemer.
33. *crystal*] crystal ball.

Guilt must not walk so near his lodge again;
He came near me now.   *Exit.*

TOMAZO.

All league with mankind I renounce forever
Till I find this murderer. Not so much
As common courtesy but I'll lock up,   45
For in the state of ignorance I live in
A brother may salute his brother's murderer
And wish good speed to th' villain in a greeting.

Enter Vermandero, Alibius, *and* Isabella.

VERMANDERO.

Noble Piracquo.

TOMAZO.   Pray keep on your way, sir;
I've nothing to say to you.

VERMANDERO.   Comforts bless you, sir.   50

TOMAZO.

I have forsworn compliment, in troth I have, sir;
As you are merely man, I have not left
A good wish for you nor any here.

VERMANDERO.

Unless you be so far in love with grief
You will not part from't upon any terms,   55
We bring that news will make a welcome for us.

TOMAZO.

What news can that be?

VERMANDERO.   Throw no scornful smile
Upon the zeal I bring you, 'tis worth more, sir;
Two of the chiefest men I kept about me
I hide not from the law or your just vengeance.   60

TOMAZO.

Ha!

VERMANDERO.

To give your peace more ample satisfaction,
Thank these discoverers.

TOMAZO.   If you bring that calm,

42. near] *Dyce*; ne're *Q.*

51. *forsworn compliment*] renounced courtesy.

Name but the manner I shall ask forgiveness in
For that contemptuous smile upon you;   65
I'll perfect it with reverence that belongs
Unto a sacred altar.   [*Kneels.*]
VERMANDERO.   Good sir, rise,   [*Raises him.*]
Why, now you overdo as much o' this hand
As you fell short o' t'other. Speak, Alibius.
ALIBIUS.
'Twas my wife's fortune, as she is most lucky   70
At a discovery, to find out lately
Within our hospital of fools and madmen
Two counterfeits slipp'd into these disguises:
Their names, Franciscus and Antonio.
VERMANDERO.
Both mine, sir, and I ask no favor for 'em.   75
ALIBIUS.
Now that which draws suspicion to their habits,
The time of their disguisings agrees justly
With the day of the murder.
TOMAZO.   Oh, blest revelation!
VERMANDERO.
Nay more, nay more, sir, I'll not spare mine own
In way of justice; they both feign'd a journey   80
To Briamata, and so wrought out their leaves;
My love was so abus'd in't.
TOMAZO.   Time's too precious
To run in waste now. You have brought a peace
The riches of five kingdoms could not purchase.
Be my most happy conduct; I thirst for 'em;   85
Like subtle lightning will I wind about 'em
And melt their marrow in 'em.   *Exeunt.*

[V.iii]   *Enter* Alsemero *and* Jasperino.
JASPERINO.
Your confidence, I'm sure, is now of proof;

---

81. *so wrought . . . leaves*] in that way worked out their requests for leave
of absence.
[V.iii]
  1. *of proof*] armored against all attacks.

The prospect from the garden has show'd
Enough for deep suspicion.
ALSEMERO.   The black mask
That so continually was worn upon't
Condemns the face for ugly ere't be seen—   5
Her despite to him and so seeming bottomless—
JASPERINO.
Touch it home then; 'tis not a shallow probe
Can search this ulcer soundly; I fear you'll find it
Full of corruption. 'Tis fit I leave you.
She meets you opportunely from that walk;   10
She took the back door at his parting with her.

                                        Exit Jasperino.

ALSEMERO.
Did my fate wait for this unhappy stroke
At my first sight of woman? She's here.

                    Enter Beatrice.

BEATRICE.
Alsemero!
ALSEMERO.   How do you?
BEATRICE.   How do I?
Alas! How do you? You look not well.   15
ALSEMERO.
You read me well enough; I am not well.
BEATRICE.
Not well, sir? Is't in my power to better you?
ALSEMERO.
Yes.
BEATRICE.   Nay then, y'are cur'd again.
ALSEMERO.
Pray resolve me one question, lady.
BEATRICE.   If I can.
ALSEMERO.
None can so sure. Are you honest?   20

---

3. *The black mask*] i.e., Beatrice's modesty and her despite to De Flores;
see note at ll. 46–51.
7. *Touch it home*] Probe it all the way to the bottom; a medical metaphor.
19. *resolve me*] settle for me.
20. *honest*] chaste.

BEATRICE.
  Ha, ha, ha, that's a broad question, my lord.
ALSEMERO.
  But that's not a modest answer, my lady.
  Do you laugh? My doubts are strong upon me.
BEATRICE.
  'Tis innocence that smiles, and no rough brow
  Can take away the dimple in her cheek.   25
  Say I should strain a tear to fill the vault,
  Which would you give the better faith to?
ALSEMERO.
  'Twere but hypocrisy of a sadder color
  But the same stuff; neither your smiles nor tears
  Shall move or flatter me from my belief: 30
  You are a whore.
BEATRICE.   What a horrid sound it hath!
  It blasts a beauty to deformity;
  Upon what face soever that breath falls
  It strikes it ugly. Oh, you have ruin'd
  What you can ne'er repair again.   35
ALSEMERO.
  I'll all demolish and seek out truth within you
  If there be any left; let your sweet tongue
  Prevent your heart's rifling; there I'll ransack
  And tear out my suspicion.
BEATRICE.   You may, sir;
  'Tis an easy passage. Yet if you please,   40
  Show me the ground whereon you lost your love;
  My spotless virtue may but tread on that
  Before I perish.
ALSEMERO.   Unanswerable:
  A ground you cannot stand on; you fall down
  Beneath all grace and goodness when you set   45
  Your ticklish heel on't. There was a visor
  O'er that cunning face and that became you;

---

26. *vault*] i.e., of the sky.
  46. *ticklish*] lascivious.
  46–51. *There . . . De Flores*] A key passage, important to the explication
of other passages in this scene. Beatrice's true face (as is now obvious) is a
"cunning face," but all this while she has concealed it by a mask ("visor")

Now impudence in triumph rides upon't.
How comes this tender reconcilement else
'Twixt you and your despite, your rancorous loathing,   50
De Flores? He that your eye was sore at sight of,
He's now become your arms' supporter, your lips' saint.

BEATRICE.
Is there the cause?

ALSEMERO.
Worse; your lust's devil, your adultery.

BEATRICE.
Would any but yourself say that   55
'Twould turn him to a villain.

ALSEMERO.   'Twas witness'd
By the counsel of your bosom, Diaphanta.

BEATRICE.
Is your witness dead, then?

ALSEMERO.   'Tis to be fear'd
It was the wages of her knowledge, poor soul;
She liv'd not long after the discovery.   60

---

of modesty which "became her" (cf. IV.ii.117–151). Now that her "cunning" has succeeded (in making Alsemero marry a whore), she has removed the becoming mask of modesty to reveal the "cunning face" of a schemer, "impudent in triumph." How can one explain this sudden change in her relationship with De Flores, her "despite" (l. 50), otherwise than by recognizing that there has been no change—that Beatrice has always been a cunning whore?

Once it is known that the modesty was only a mask (one characterized also by a disgust of De Flores), then (1) it must have been worn for purposes of hypocritical deceit and it may be termed "black" (l. 3), for the color of all hypocrisy is "sad" (l. 28), and consequently (2) whatever face the mask covered with its deception must be "ugly" (ll. 5, 199); no face lovely in its genuineness would wear a mask. Hence one may condemn that genuine face "for ugly" even though he has never seen it (l. 5). How can one explain "her despite to [De Flores] and so seeming bottomless" (l. 6) otherwise than by recognizing that it has all been hypocritical "seeming" or "close disguise" (l. 129)?

In short, all men are "blind" (l. 110) before the hypocrisy of women; as far as they can see, "fair-fac'd saints" (l. 110) are indistinguishable from "cunning devils" (l. 109) or "crying crocodiles" (l. 113).

52. *arms' supporter*] (1) the man or beast that stands beside the shield of arms in heraldic blazoning (cf. earlier comment on Beatrice's descent: III.iv.135–137); (2) the physical sustainer of your body as he is the spiritual sustainer to whom the prayers of your spirit are voiced.

BEATRICE.

    Then hear a story of not much less horror
    Than this your false suspicion is beguil'd with.
    To your bed's scandal I stand up innocent
    Which even the guilt of one black other deed
    Will stand for proof of: your love has made me   65
    A cruel murderess.

ALSEMERO.   Ha!

BEATRICE.   A bloody one.

    I have kiss'd poison for't, strok'd a serpent,
    That thing of hate, worthy in my esteem
    Of no better employment; and him most worthy
    To be so employ'd, I caus'd to murder   70
    That innocent Piracquo, having no
    Better means than that worst to assure
    Yourself to me.

ALSEMERO.   Oh, the place itself e'er since
    Has crying been for vengeance, the temple
    Where blood and beauty first unlawfully   75
    Fir'd their devotion and quench'd the right one.
    'Twas in my fears at first, 'twill have it now;
    Oh, thou art all deform'd.

BEATRICE.   Forget not, sir,

    It for your sake was done; shall greater dangers
    Make the less welcome?

ALSEMERO.   Oh, thou shouldst have gone   80
    A thousand leagues about to have avoided
    This dangerous bridge of blood; here we are lost.

BEATRICE.

    Remember I am true unto your bed.

ALSEMERO.

    The bed itself's a charnel, the sheets shrouds
    For murdered carcasses; it must ask pause   85
    What I must do in this; meantime you shall

63. innocent] *this edn.*; innocence
Q. See Appendix A.

---

73. *the place*] the temple.
77. *it*] i.e., vengeance.
81. *about*] around; i.e., a detour.

Be my prisoner only: enter my closet;   *Exit* Beatrice.
I'll be your keeper yet. Oh, in what part
Of this sad story shall I first begin?
                    Enter De Flores.
                                        Ha!
This same fellow has put me in. De Flores.   90
DE FLORES.
    Noble Alsemero.
ALSEMERO.   I can tell you
News, sir; my wife has her commended to you.
DE FLORES.
    That's news indeed, my lord; I think she would
    Commend me to the gallows if she could,
    She ever lov'd me so well, I thank her.   95
ALSEMERO.
    What's this blood upon your band, De Flores?
DE FLORES.
    Blood? No, sure 'twas wash'd since.
ALSEMERO.   Since when, man?
DE FLORES.
    Since t'other day I got a knock
    In a sword and dagger school; I think 'tis out.
ALSEMERO.
    Yes, 'tis almost out, but 'tis perceiv'd, though.   100
    I had forgot my message; this it is:
    What price goes murder?
DE FLORES.   How, sir?
ALSEMERO.   I ask you, sir.
    My wife's behindhand with you, she tells me,
    For a brave, bloody blow you gave for her sake
    Upon Piracquo.
DE FLORES.   Upon? 'Twas quite through him, sure.   105
    Has she confess'd it?
ALSEMERO.   As sure as death to both of you,

89. S.D.] *after l.* 90 *in* Q.

---

    90. *put me in*] i.e., put me in mind (put in my mind) where I shall first
begin.
    96. *band*] neckband.
    103. *behindhand*] slow in making payment.

And much more than that.

DE FLORES.   It could not be much more;
'Twas but one thing, and that she's a whore.

ALSEMERO.

It could not choose but follow; oh, cunning devils!
How should blind men know you from fair-fac'd saints?   110

BEATRICE (*within*).

He lies, the villain does belie me.

DE FLORES.

Let me go to her, sir.

ALSEMERO.   Nay, you shall to her.
Peace, crying crocodile, your sounds are heard;
Take your prey to you. Get you in to her, sir.   *Exit* De Flores.
I'll be your pander now; rehearse again   115
Your scene of lust, that you may be perfect
When you shall come to act it to the black audience
Where howls and gnashings shall be music to you.
Clip your adulteress freely; 'tis the pilot
Will guide you to the *Mare Mortuum*   120
Where you shall sink to fathoms bottomless.

Enter Vermandero, Alibius, Isabella, Tomazo, Franciscus, *and* Antonio.

VERMANDERO.

Oh, Alsemero, I have a wonder for you.

ALSEMERO.

No, sir, 'tis I, I have a wonder for you.

VERMANDERO.

I have suspicion near as proof itself
For Piracquo's murder.

ALSEMERO.   Sir, I have proof   125
Beyond suspicion for Piracquo's murder.

VERMANDERO.

Beseech you, hear me; these two have been disguis'd

109. It] *Dilke*; I *Q*.

---

110. *blind men*] i.e., blind man; see note at ll. 46–51.

113. *crying crocodile*] The crocodile was thought to shed tears in order to delude its victims; see note at ll. 46–51.

119. *Clip*] embrace.

120. *Mare Mortuum*] the Dead Sea, thought to be bottomless; perhaps it suggests the "bottomless pit of hell" (Bawcutt).

E'er since the deed was done.

ALSEMERO.   I have two other
That were more close disguis'd than your two could be
E'er since the deed was done.   130

VERMANDERO.

You'll hear me, these mine own servants—

ALSEMERO.

Hear me, those nearer than your servants
That shall acquit them and prove them guiltless.

FRANCISCUS.

That may be done with easy truth, sir.

TOMAZO.

How is my cause bandied through your delays!   135
'Tis urgent in blood and calls for haste;
Give me a brother alive or dead:
Alive, a wife with him; if dead, for both
A recompense for murder and adultery.

BEATRICE (within).

Oh, oh, oh.

ALSEMERO.   Hark, 'tis coming to you.   140

DE FLORES (within).

Nay, I'll along for company.

BEATRICE (within).   Oh, oh.

VERMANDERO.

What horrid sounds are these?

ALSEMERO.

Come forth, you twins of mischief.

Enter De Flores *bringing in* Beatrice.

DE FLORES.

Here we are; if you have any more
To say to us, speak quickly; I shall not   145
Give you the hearing else; I am so stout yet
And so I think that broken rib of mankind.

VERMANDERO.

An host of enemies enter'd my citadel

---

135. *bandied*] tossed back and forth as if a tennis ball.
147. *broken . . . mankind*] woman; alluding to her creation from Adam's
rib.

Could not amaze like this. Joanna, Beatrice Joanna.

BEATRICE.

Oh, come not near me, sir; I shall defile you.   150
I am that of your blood was taken from you
For your better health; look no more upon't
But cast it to the ground regardlessly.
Let the common sewer take it from distinction.
Beneath the stars, upon yon meteor   155
Ever hung my fate 'mongst things corruptible;
I ne'er could pluck it from him. My loathing
Was prophet to the rest but ne'er believ'd;
Mine honor fell with him and now my life.
Alsemero, I am a stranger to your bed;   160
Your bed was cozen'd on the nuptial night
For which your false bride died.

ALSEMERO.   Diaphanta!

DE FLORES.

Yes, and the while I coupled with your mate
At barley-break; now we are left in hell.

VERMANDERO.

We are all there, it circumscribes here.   165

DE FLORES.

I lov'd this woman in spite of her heart;
Her love I earn'd out of Piracquo's murder.

TOMAZO.

Ha, my brother's murderer.

DE FLORES.   Yes, and her honor's prize
Was my reward. I thank life for nothing
But that pleasure; it was so sweet to me   170
That I have drunk up all, left none behind

156. hung] *Dyce*; hang *Q*.

---

154. *from distinction*] away from its state of being distinct.

155–156. *Beneath . . . corruptible*] According to medieval astrology, the stars governed the fate of men or represented their guardian angels; they were unchanging and incorruptible. Beatrice's fate depended on a meteor (far beneath the stars—sublunary, in fact), changing and corruptible.

164. *barley-break*] see note to III.iii.162.

165. *circumscribes*] i.e., the central circle ("hell") of the game of barley-break.

For any man to pledge me.
VERMANDERO.   Horrid villain!
Keep life in him for further tortures.
DE FLORES.   No;
   I can prevent you, here's my penknife still.
   It is but one thread more, [*stabs himself*] and now 'tis cut.   175
   Make haste, Joanna, by that token to thee
   Canst not forget so lately put in mind;
   I would not go to leave thee far behind.   *Dies.*
BEATRICE.
   Forgive me, Alsemero, all forgive;
   'Tis time to die, when 'tis a shame to live.   *Dies.* 180
VERMANDERO.
   Oh, my name is enter'd now in that record
   Where till this fatal hour 'twas never read.
ALSEMERO.
   Let it be blotted out; let your heart lose it,
   And it can never look you in the face
   Nor tell a tale behind the back of life   185
   To your dishonor. Justice hath so right
   The guilty hit, that innocence is quit
   By proclamation and may joy again.
   Sir, you are sensible of what truth hath done;
   'Tis the best comfort that your grief can find.   190
TOMAZO.
   Sir, I am satisfied; my injuries
   Lie dead before me. I can exact no more,
   Unless my soul were loose and could o'ertake
   Those black fugitives, that are fled from thence,
   To take a second vengeance; but there are wraths   195
   Deeper than mine ('tis to be fear'd) about 'em.
ALSEMERO.
   What an opacous body had that moon
   That last chang'd on us! Here's beauty chang'd
   To ugly whoredom; here servant obedience

---

172. *pledge*] toast.
176. *token*] i.e., the wound he has just given himself.
181. *record*] "the heavenly record of human deeds" (Bawcutt).
194. *black fugitives*] sin-black flying souls.
197 *opacous*] darkened, obscure, therefore ominous or malevolent.

To a master sin, imperious murder.   200
I, a suppos'd husband, chang'd embraces
With wantonness, but that was paid before;
Your change is come, too, from an ignorant wrath
To knowing friendship. Are there any more on's?

ANTONIO.

Yes, sir, I was chang'd too from a little ass as I was to a great 205
fool as I am, and had like to ha' been chang'd to the gallows
but that you know my innocence always excuses me.

FRANCISCUS.

I was chang'd from a little wit to be stark mad, almost for
the same purpose.

ISABELLA.

Your change is still behind,   210
But deserve best your transformation;
You are a jealous coxcomb, keep schools of folly,
And teach your scholars how to break your own head.

ALIBIUS.

I see all apparent, wife, and will change now
Into a better husband, and never keep   215
Scholars that shall be wiser than myself.

ALSEMERO.

Sir, you have yet a son's duty living,
Please you accept it; let that your sorrow,
As it goes from your eye, go from your heart;
Man and his sorrow at the grave must part.   220

Epilogue

ALSEMERO.

All we can do to comfort one another,
To stay a brother's sorrow for a brother,
To dry a child from the kind father's eyes,
Is to no purpose; it rather multiplies.
Your only smiles have power to cause relive   5

---

207. *innocence*] (1) guiltlessness; (2) "temporary insanity."
210. *still behind*] still to come.
213. *break . . . head*] i.e., with cuckold's horns.
[Epilogue]
5. *Your . . . smiles*] Only your smiles.

The dead again or in their rooms to give
Brother a new brother, father a child:
If these appear, all griefs are reconcil'd.   *Exeunt omnes.*

FINIS

Appendix A

Supplementary Textual Notes

I.i.113. *found*] Bawcutt's defense of the Q "sound" provides an unconvincing reading: "Almost every man in a thousand healthy people is unhealthy." The thousand thus cannot be sound.

I.ii.121. *I warrant you I'll make*] I suggest that the Q "Ile warrant you make," obviously corrupt, results from compositorial anticipation.

II.ii.41. *too blame*] This construction, historically the dative infinitive, was misconstrued in the sixteenth and seventeenth centuries; "to" was spelled "too" and "blame" was taken as an adjective (*OED*, "blame," 6). The form occurs also at III.iv.97 and in Middleton's *A Mad World, My Masters* (I.ii.144).

IV.iii.1. *waxing*] The Q "waiting" is incomprehensible, and Dilke's emendation to "waning" seems to pervert the meaning. "Waxing" is what the sense requires, and the misreading of *x* as two minims (here *it*) though rare (as, of course, the letter *x* is) is possible, one form of the secretary *x* consisting of no more than two minims (see Leon Kellner, *Restoring Shakespeare* [Leipzig], 1925, § 126: *King Lear*, IV. iv. 2, Q "vent," F "vext"). Mr. Robert Krueger has pointed out to me that of these two minims the stroke on the right was usually the longer. Such a stroke might easily be mistaken for the staff of an uncrossed *t*; if the terminal *g* was topped with a long stroke, that stroke might have been mistaken for the crossing of a *t*, thus confirming the compositor in his error.

V.iii.63. *innocent*] The Q "innocence" depends almost certainly on the common misreading of *t* as *c* (see Kellner, *Restoring Shakespeare*, § 68, for many examples). "Stand up [=set up, put forward] innocence" requires transitive force to the verb, a usage that the *OED* does not recognize before the nineteenth century.

Appendix B

Chronology

Approximate years are indicated by *, occurrences in doubt by (?).

Political and Literary Events	Life and Major Works of Middleton and Rowley

1558
Accession of Queen Elizabeth I.
Robert Greene born.
Thomas Kyd born.

1560
George Chapman born.

1561
Francis Bacon born.

1564
Shakespeare born.
Christopher Marlowe born.

1570
Thomas Heywood born.*

1572
Thomas Dekker born.*
John Donne born.
Massacre of St. Bartholomew's Day.

1573
Ben Jonson born.*

1576
The Theatre, the first permanent public theater in London, established by James Burbage.
John Marston born.

1577
The Curtain theater opened.
Holinshed's *Chronicles of England, Scotland and Ireland*.
Drake begins circumnavigation of the earth; completed 1580.

1578
John Lyly's *Euphues: The Anatomy of Wit.*
1579
John Fletcher born.
Sir Thomas North's translation of Plutarch's *Lives.*
1580

Thomas Middleton born in London, baptized April 18.

1583
Philip Massinger born.
1584
Francis Beaumont born.*
1585

William Rowley born.*

1586
Death of Sir Philip Sidney.
John Ford born.
1587
The Rose theater opened by Henslowe.
Marlowe's *TAMBURLAINE*, Part I.*
Execution of Mary, Queen of Scots.
Drake raids Cadiz.
1588
Defeat of the Spanish Armada.
Marlowe's *TAMBURLAINE*, Part II.*
1589
Greene's *FRIAR BACON AND FRIAR BUNGAY.**
Marlowe's *THE JEW OF MALTA.**
Kyd's *THE SPANISH TRAGEDY.**
1590
Spenser's *Faerie Queene* (Books I–III) published.
Sidney's *Arcadia* published.
Shakespeare's *HENRY VI*, Parts I–III,* *TITUS ANDRONICUS.**
1591
Shakespeare's *RICHARD III.**
1592
Marlowe's *DOCTOR FAUSTUS** and *EDWARD II.**

Shakespeare's *TAMING OF THE SHREW** and *THE COMEDY OF ERRORS.**
Death of Greene.

1593
Shakespeare's *LOVE'S LABOR'S LOST;** *Venus and Adonis* published.
Death of Marlowe.
Theaters closed on account of plague.

1594
Shakespeare's *TWO GENTLEMEN OF VERONA;** *The Rape of Lucrece* published.
Shakespeare's company becomes Lord Chamberlain's Men.
Death of Kyd.

1595
The Swan theater built.
Sidney's *Defense of Poesy* published.
Shakespeare's *ROMEO AND JULIET,** *A MIDSUMMER NIGHT'S DREAM,** *RICHARD II.**
Raleigh's first expedition to Guiana.

1596
Spenser's *Faerie Queene* (Books IV–VI) published.
Shakespeare's *MERCHANT OF VENICE,** *KING JOHN.**
James Shirley born.

1597
Bacon's *Essays* (first edition).
Shakespeare's *HENRY IV*, Part I.*

Middleton's first published verse, *The Wisdom of Solomon Paraphrased.*

1598
Demolition of The Theatre.
Shakespeare's *MUCH ADO ABOUT NOTHING,** *HENRY IV*, Part II.*
Jonson's *EVERY MAN IN HIS HUMOR* (first version).
Seven books of Chapman's translation of Homer's *Iliad* published.

Middleton matriculated at Queen's College, Oxford, April 9.

1599
The Paul's Boys reopen their theater.
The Globe theater opened.

Middleton's *Micro-Cynicon* (poem) published.

Shakespeare's *AS YOU LIKE IT*,*
*HENRY V, JULIUS CAESAR.**
Marston's *ANTONIO AND MEL-*
*LIDA.** Parts I and II.
Dekker's *THE SHOEMAKERS'*
*HOLIDAY.**
Death of Spenser.

1600

Shakespeare's *TWELFTH*
*NIGHT.**
The Fortune theater built by Alleyn.
The Children of the Chapel begin
to play at the Blackfriars.

Middleton's *Ghost of Lucrece* (poem)
published.

1601

Shakespeare's *HAMLET*,* *MERRY*
*WIVES OF WINDSOR.**
Insurrection and execution of the
Earl of Essex.
Jonson's *POETASTER.*

1602

Shakespeare's *TROILUS AND*
*CRESSIDA.**

Middleton married to Mary (or
Magdalen) Marbeck.*
Middleton's *THE CHESTER*
TRAGEDY, OR RANDALL EARL
OF CHESTER (lost) and *THE*
*FAMILY OF LOVE** (both for the
Admiral's Men); *BLURT MAS-*
TER CONSTABLE (Paul's Boys);
Middleton, Dekker, Drayton, Mun-
day, and Webster's *CAESAR'S*
FALL (lost) (Admiral's Men).
December 14, receives 5s. for a
prologue and epilogue for a court
performance of *FRIAR BACON*
AND FRIAR BUNGAY.

1603

Death of Queen Elizabeth I; acces-
sion of James VI of Scotland as
James I.
Florio's translation of Montaigne's
Essays published.
Shakespeare's *ALL'S WELL THAT*
*ENDS WELL.**
Heywood's *A WOMAN KILLED*
WITH KINDNESS.
Marston's *THE MALCONTENT.**
Shakespeare's company becomes
the King's Men.

Middleton's *THE PHOENIX**
(Paul's Boys).
The True Narration of the Entertain-
ment of His Royal Majesty from
Edinburgh till London (pamphlet), by
Middleton.

1604

Shakespeare's *MEASURE FOR MEASURE,* OTHELLO.*
Marston's *THE FAWN.*
Chapman's *BUSSY D'AMBOIS.*

Middleton's son Edward born.*
Middleton published two pamphlets, *The Ant and the Nightingale, or Father Hubburd's Tales* and *The Black Book.*
Middleton's *THE PURITAN, OR THE WIDOW OF WATLING STREET*(?)*(Paul's Boys); Middleton and Dekker's *THE HONEST WHORE*, Part I (Prince Henry's Men).

1605

Shakespeare's *KING LEAR.*
Marston's *THE DUTCH COURTESAN.*
Bacon's *Advancement of Learning* published.
The Gunpowder Plot.

Middleton's *MICHAELMAS TERM*; *A MAD WORLD, MY MASTERS*; *A TRICK TO CATCH THE OLD ONE* (all Paul's Boys).

1606

Shakespeare's *MACBETH.*
Jonson's *VOLPONE.*
Tourneur's *REVENGER'S TRAGEDY.*
The Red Bull theater built.
Death of John Lyly.

Middleton's *THE VIPER AND HER BROOD* (lost).

1607

Shakespeare's *ANTONY AND CLEOPATRA.*
Beaumont's *KNIGHT OF THE BURNING PESTLE.*
Settlement of Jamestown, Virginia.

Rowley, Day, and Wilkins' *THE TRAVELS OF THREE ENGLISH BROTHERS.*
Middleton's *YOUR FIVE GALLANTS* (Children of the Chapel).

1608

Shakespeare's *CORIOLANUS,* TIMON OF ATHENS.* PERICLES.*
Chapman's *CONSPIRACY AND TRAGEDY OF CHARLES, DUKE OF BYRON.*
Dekker's *Gull's Hornbook* published.
Richard Burbage leases Blackfriars Theatre for King's company.
John Milton born.

Rowley's *A SHOEMAKER A GENTLEMAN* and (with Heywood) *FORTUNE BY LAND AND SEA* (Queen's Men).
Middleton and Dekker's *THE ROARING GIRL* (Prince Henry's Men).

1609

Shakespeare's *CYMBELINE;* Sonnets* published.
Jonson's *EPICOENE.*

Rowley began his acting career with Prince Charles's Men.
Rowley's *A Search for Money* (pamphlet). Middleton's *Sir Robert Sherley's Entertainment in Cracovia* (pamphlet).

1610

Jonson's *ALCHEMIST*.
Chapman's *REVENGE OF BUSSY D'AMBOIS*.*
Richard Crashaw born.

Rowley's *A NEW WONDER, A WOMAN NEVER VEXED*.

1611

Authorized (King James) Version of the Bible published.
Shakespeare's *THE WINTER'S TALE*,* *THE TEMPEST*.*
Beaumont and Fletcher's *A KING AND NO KING*.
Tourneur's *ATHEIST'S TRAGEDY*.*
Chapman's translation of *Iliad* completed.

Middleton's *A CHASTE MAID IN CHEAPSIDE** (Princess Elizabeth's Men); *THE SECOND MAIDEN'S TRAGEDY*(?)*.
Middleton and Rowley's *WIT AT SEVERAL WEAPONS*(?)*.

1612

Webster's *THE WHITE DEVIL*.*

Rowley's *HYMEN'S HOLIDAYS OR CUPID'S VAGARIES* (lost).
Middleton's *NO WIT, NO HELP LIKE A WOMAN'S* (Princess Elizabeth's Men [?]).

1613

The Globe theater burned.
Shakespeare's *HENRY VIII* (with Fletcher).
Webster's *THE DUCHESS OF MALFI*.*
Sir Thomas Overbury murdered.

Rowley's *A KNAVE IN PRINT* (lost) and *THE FOOL WITHOUT BOOK* (lost).
Middleton began his career of writing for civic and official ceremonies with *THE NEW RIVER ENTERTAINMENT* and *THE TRIUMPHS OF TRUTH*, the latter for the election and establishment of Sir Thomas Middleton as Lord Mayor of London.

1614

The Globe theater rebuilt.
The Hope Theatre built.
Jonson's *BARTHOLOMEW FAIR*.

Middleton's *THE MASQUE OF CUPID* (lost).

1615

Middleton's *THE WITCH** and *MORE DISSEMBLERS BESIDES WOMEN** (both King's Men).

1616

Publication of Folio edition of Jonson's *Works*.
Chapman's *Whole Works of Homer*.
Death of Shakespeare.
Death of Beaumont.

Middleton's *THE MAYOR OF QUINBOROUGH OR HENGIST KING OF KENT**; *THE WIDOW**; *THE NICE VALOR** with Fletcher (?) (all King's Men). Middleton's *CIVITATIS AMOR* for the reception of Charles on his creation as Prince of Wales.

1617

Middleton and Rowley's *A FAIR QUARREL* (Prince Charles's Men). Middleton's *THE TRIUMPHS OF HONOR AND INDUSTRY*, for the Company of Grocers on the establishment of one of their number as Lord Mayor.

1618

Outbreak of Thirty Years War.
Execution of Raleigh.

Middleton, Massinger, and Rowley's *THE OLD LAW** (King's Men [?]).
Middleton's *The Peacemaker* (pamphlet).

1619

Middleton's *INNER TEMPLE MASQUE OR MASQUE OF HEROES* (Prince Charles's Men, with Rowley playing Plumporridge). Rowley's *ALL'S LOST BY LUST* (Prince Charles's Men, with Rowley playing Jacques). Middleton and Rowley's *THE WORLD TOSSED AT TENNIS* (Prince Charles's Men, with Rowley playing Simplicity). Middleton's *THE TRIUMPHS OF LOVE AND ANTIQUITY*, for the establishment of the Lord Mayor, and *On the Death of Richard Burbage* (elegy).

1620

Settlement of Plymouth, Massachusetts.

Middleton appointed City Chronologer, September 6, with the duty of writing the annual chronology of the City of London.
Middleton's *The Marriage of the Old and New Testament* (?) (pamphlet).
Rowley's *THE BIRTH OF MERLIN*.

1621

Robert Burton's *Anatomy of Melancholy* published.
Andrew Marvell born.

Rowley, Ford, and Dekker's *THE WITCH OF EDMONTON* (Prince Charles's Men).
Middleton and Webster's (?) *ANYTHING FOR A QUIET LIFE**; Middleton's *WOMEN BEWARE WOMEN** (King's Men).
Middleton and Munday's *THE SUN IN ARIES* (?), for the Company of Drapers at the establishment of the Lord Mayor; and nine *HONORABLE ENTERTAINMENTS*.

1622

Henry Vaughan born.

Middleton and Rowley's *THE CHANGELING* (Princess Elizabeth's Men).
Rowley's *A MATCH AT MIDNIGHT* (Children of the Revels).
Middleton's *AN INVENTION FOR THE LORD MAYOR*, for the Lord Mayor's feast; and *THE TRIUMPHS OF HONOUR AND VIRTUE*, for the Company of Grocers at the establishment of the Lord Mayor.

1623

Publication of Folio edition of Shakespeare's *COMEDIES, HISTORIES, AND TRAGEDIES*.

Rowley joins the King's Men as an actor.
Middleton and Rowley's *THE SPANISH GYPSY* (Princess Elizabeth's Men); *THE TRIUMPHS OF INTEGRITY*, for the Company of Drapers at the establishment of the Lord Mayor.
Rowley and Fletcher's *THE MAID IN THE MILL* (King's Men).

1624

Middleton's *A GAME AT CHESS* (King's Men, with Rowley playing the Fat Bishop [the Archbishop of Spalatro]).
Rowley, Ford, Dekker, and Webster's *KEEP THE WIDOW WAKING* (lost).

APPENDIX B

1625
Death of King James I; accession
of Charles I.
Death of Fletcher.

Rowley and Webster's *A CURE FOR
A CUCKOLD*.

1626
Death of Tourneur.
Death of Bacon.

Rowley buried at Clerkenwell.
Middleton's *THE TRIUMPHS OF
HEALTH AND PROSPERITY*, for
the Company of Drapers at the
establishment of the Lord Mayor.

1627

Middleton buried at Newington
Butts, July 4.

1628
Ford's *THE LOVER'S MELAN-
CHOLY*.
Petition of Right.
Buckingham assassinated.

1631
Shirley's *THE TRAITOR*.
Death of Donne.
John Dryden born.

1632
Massinger's *THE CITY MADAM*.*

1633
Donne's *Poems* published.
Death of George Herbert.

1634
Death of Chapman, Marston, Web-
ster.*
Publication of *THE TWO NOBLE
KINSMEN*, with title-page attribu-
tion to Shakespeare and Fletcher.
Milton's *Comus*.

1635
Sir Thomas Browne's *Religio Medici*.

1637
Death of Jonson.

1639
First Bishops' War.
Death of Carew.*

1640
Short Parliament.
Long Parliament impeaches Laud.
Death of Massinger, Burton.

1641
Irish rebel.
Death of Heywood.

1642
Charles I leaves London; Civil War breaks out.
Shirley's *COURT SECRET*.
All theaters closed by Act of Parliament.

1643
Parliament swears to the Solemn League and Covenant.

1645
Ordinance for New Model Army enacted.

1646
End of First Civil War.

1647
Army occupies London.
Charles I forms alliance with Scots.
Publication of Folio edition of Beaumont and Fletcher's *COMEDIES AND TRAGEDIES*.